The Chinese Enterprise Globalization Series

Series Editors

Huiyao Wang, Center for China and Globalization, Beijing, Beijing, China

Lu Miao, Center for China and Globalization, Beijing, China

This series contributes to the field of globalization and Chinese enterprises studies. It publishes completely up-to-date monographs dedicated to this topic. It also provides a wealth of the latest information regarding Chinese ODI. In addition to this data, the series stands head and shoulders above other work in this area due to its in-depth case studies on Chinese companies going global, all of which are based on thorough primary research.

The key words in TCEGS include but are not limited to:

- Going global
- Globalization
- ODI
- FDI
- Cross-border M&A
- One Belt One Road
- International talent
- Risks
- Challenges
- Outbound Investment
- Chinese enterprises
- Greenfield investment

More information about this series at http://www.springer.com/series/16146

Huiyao Wang · Lu Miao

The Globalization of Chinese Enterprises: Trends and Characteristics

Springer

Huiyao Wang
Center for China and Globalization
Beijing, China

Lu Miao
Center for China and Globalization
Beijing, China

ISSN 2524-5929 ISSN 2524-5937 (electronic)
The Chinese Enterprise Globalization Series
ISBN 978-981-15-4645-7 ISBN 978-981-15-4646-4 (eBook)
https://doi.org/10.1007/978-981-15-4646-4

This Springer imprint is published by the registered company Springer Nature Singapore Pte Ltd.
The registered company address is: 152 Beach Road, #21-01/04 Gateway East, Singapore 189721, Singapore

Foreword by Yongtu Long

Perseverance: The Challenging Path to Globalization for Chinese Enterprises

In 2017, the world economy entered a state of stable recovery. However, due to rising anti-globalization and trade protectionism, FDI dropped drastically worldwide, decreasing by 23% to $1.43 trillion. As a key participant in the international economy, in 2017, Chinese enterprises' OFDI declined for the first time in more than 10 years, with China moving from the second largest source of FDI worldwide in 2016 to third largest in 2017. While Chinese enterprises' FDI decreased, China also faced increasing trade conflicts with other countries. Since Donald Trump became US president, Sino-US trade relations have seen increasing tensions. As a result, since March 2018, both China and the US have adopted anti-dumping policies and increased tariffs on commodities. The "trade frictions" between China and America has cast a shadow over the global economy, impacting companies and ordinary citizens in both countries, leading to stock market falls and market panic. Given this backdrop, questions have arisen regarding China's engagement in global markets and the globalization of Chinese enterprises: Was it right for China to join the WTO? What is the future for China's outbound trade? Should China continue to support economic globalization? Should Chinese enterprises maintain their "go global" strategies and if so, how can they succeed?

Uncertainties always undermine the confidence to move forward. Nonetheless, we should focus on the entire development process and its underlying logic rather than just superficial phenomena. 2018 marks the 40th anniversary of China's Reform and Opening-Up policy, the 18th anniversary of China joining the WTO, as well as an important legislative year in China for deepening comprehensive reform. Therefore, during this critical year, it is helpful to review the history and look into the future of Chinese enterprise globalization, analyzing current challenges and opportunities.

In Retrospect: 40 Years of Chinese Enterprise Globalization

The "go global" strategy has been central to the globalization of Chinese enterprises. During the 30 years from the establishment of the People's Republic of China to 1978, some Chinese enterprises did engage in limited outbound investment. Although these enterprises' overseas branches were small scale and developed slowly; they became the seed of the "go global" wave to come, providing valuable experience and a foundation for Chinese firms' globalization strategies in the Reform and Opening-up period. In retrospect, the 40 years of Reform and Opening-up is the crucial stage in the history of Chinese enterprises. From their origins as local companies, Chinese enterprises have transformed into an important force and proponent of economic globalization. To formulate suggestions for the current set of challenges faced by Chinese enterprises, a review of the historical process of the globalization of Chinese enterprises is in order.

The first phase marks the initial development of Chinese enterprise globalization, starting with the Third Plenary Session of the 11th Central Committee held in 1978. At this meeting, Chinese leaders announced the launch of Reform and Opening-up. Following that, a series of policies and regulations beneficial to economic development were steadily introduced. During this period, domestic enterprises were allowed to invest and build in other countries. In 1979, the State Council promulgated 15 economic reform policies. The 13th policy in this series of new policies stated that "companies are allowed to build factories in foreign countries," which was official approval for enterprises to "go global." Since then, based on their operational experience since the establishment of the PRC and their determination to expand overseas, the first wave of Chinese enterprises started to expand their overseas presence, including companies such as China National Chemicals Import and Export Corporation, China National Metals and Minerals Import and Export Corporation, and Shanghai Machinery Import and Export Corporation. By 1992, there were 4117 Chinese corporations operating across more than 120 countries and regions, including joint ventures, single proprietorship and cooperative companies, with total investment amounting to $3.204 billion.

The second phase saw an adjustment of Chinese enterprises' "go global" policies. From 1993, China decided to change its economic structure and implemented contractionary monetary policies to help ensure a soft-landing for the overheated economy. This saw the "go global" movement of Chinese enterprises enter a stage of structural adjustment and rectification, causing a slowing of globalization process. From 1993 to 1998, the OFDI of Chinese enterprises came to $1.278 billion, and 1500 new companies started businesses in foreign countries. The scope of Chinese OFDI extended to the development of foreign resources and manufacturing and processing industries, as well as import and export trade, engineering contracting, consulting services and other tertiary industries.

At the time, the general international consensus supported economic globalization. As the global economy was significantly more developed than most Chinese enterprises, China recognized the gap and set future policy direction accordingly. Therefore, reviewing experiences from this period, the Chinese government proposed developing industries with comparative advantages and attached more importance to the "go global" strategy of state-owned enterprises (SOEs). The Chinese government also resolved that overseas Chinese enterprises should receive support from both foreign and domestic markets and resources.

The third stage saw rapid development in the globalization of Chinese enterprises. With WTO entry in 2001, China saw rapid growth in not only inbound but also outbound investment. WTO membership accelerated China's integration into the world economy. This not only enabled the development of China's economy, but also propelled global growth and globalization. However, new global opportunities for Chinese firms also came with challenges.

In terms of opportunities, China's participation in the WTO was advantageous to the entire world economy. At that time, China functioned as the "world's factory," producing high-quality products at a low cost. In effect, this economic activity constituted a massive poverty alleviation project. After 18 years in the WTO, the Chinese people had broadened their horizons, liberated productive forces for outbound trade, and realized greater development through Reform and Opening-up.

In terms of challenges, while most countries continued to strive for free trade, flaws in WTO rules saw that trade protectionism became increasingly pervasive. Countries often adopted policies that, while not directly contradicting WTO rules, became commonly used for protectionist ends. After China joined the WTO, developed countries adopted protectionist measures such as anti-dumping and anti-subsidy investigations in sectors in which China enjoyed advantages brought by its cheap and large labor force.

Today, with China's growing scientific and technological strength and its gradual climbing of the industrial chain, developed countries have begun to target China with investigations on issues such as technical barriers, intellectual property protection and environmental barriers. However, despite encountering difficulties in 18 years in the WTO, China has become the third largest source of OFDI and the second largest inbound destination for FDI, demonstrating China's rise and economic significance.

Strategic Games: Friction in the Globalization of Chinese Enterprises

In March 2018, the US launched a series of high tariffs on Chinese exports, making Sino-US economic relations a global issue. However, the impact of current trade frictions should not be exaggerated. Overly downbeat predictions of the "trade frictions" do nothing but spread panic and pessimism, and are likely to lead to falls in the stock market.

Since China joined the WTO in 2001, there have been lots of so-called anti-dumping and anti-subsidy "trade frictions" between China and America. Yet, this did not halt the growth of either the global economy or global trade. Current frictions can be seen as a result of market behavior and an escalation of continuing trade tensions.

In 2009, the US International Trade Commission sought to impose special tariffs on China of 55, 45 and 35% respectively over 3 consecutive years, arguing that China was attempting to disrupt the US market. In October 2010, US Trade Representatives announced that in response to a petition from United Steelworkers, the official representative body of the US steel industry, the US would launch "301 investigations" against a series of China's energy policies. Ultimately, China and the US settled these disputes under the WTO dispute settlement mechanism.

In 2012, President Obama blocked investment in US wind power projects by firms affiliated to China's Sany Heavy Industry. The same year, the US Congress denied market access for two Chinese communication companies, Huawei and ZTE. Since 2018, the US Department of Commerce has levied several tariffs on Chinese exports, including a 106.09% tariff on aluminum foil, a 25% tariff on steel, and a 109.95% tariff on sewage pipeline accessories. US trade protectionist policies have caused losses and put up barriers to the globalization of Chinese enterprises. Since Donald Trump assumed office, his unpredictable style has caused much concern for Chinese investors. However, given the Trump administration's "America First" stance and emphasis on reducing the US trade deficit, the imposition of tariffs targeting China did not come as a surprise.

When dealing with trade disputes, it takes a rational mindset and pragmatic, prudent approach to find resolutions. The reduction of the trade deficit is a progressive process which ultimately must be solved by market forces. Sole reliance on administrative measures and combative trade policies is not an effective way to solve the dispute. To date, current Chinese countermeasures to the US have been restrained, indicating that China wants to leave room for future negotiations. This is an important principle that must be borne in mind when tackling significant international trade issues. The current trade frictions between China and the US represent a major change in US strategy towards China, with the potential to lead to a series of subsequent misjudgments. From the perspective of global supply chains, American consumers and businesses who work with Chinese partners share considerable interests with China. Therefore, there is ample room for both sides to negotiate.

Looking Forward: The Future Globalization of Chinese Enterprises

It has been 40 years since the start of China's Reform and Opening-Up and 18 years since WTO entry. Over this time, Chinese enterprises have made considerable progress. According to the latest data, in 2017, China's imports and exports amounted to CNY 27.79 trillion, a 14.2% increase from the previous year. This growth further solidifies China's position as a leading trading nation. During this time, globalizing Chinese enterprises have overcome challenges, seized opportunities and played to their advantages.

In 2013, President Xi Jinping launched the Belt and Road Initiative (BRI). The BRI serves as a new platform for Chinese enterprises to globalize and creates new opportunities for integration of the world economy. For Chinese enterprises to grasp the opportunities the BRI offers and improve FDI and sustainable development, wide-ranging and multi-level cooperation with other countries and regions in all aspects along the BRI must be strengthened. Moreover, Chinese enterprises should look to undertake practical projects that benefit local people and have popular support. By doing so, Chinese companies can enhance their international reach and credibility. Both state-owned and private companies have the chance to play a meaningful role in the BRI's development. They should seek to deepen their sense of social participation and responsibility to win trust and respect in new markets. State-owned companies, which are more resilient to risk, can look to undertake projects in politically and institutionally underdeveloped countries and regions. As a catalyst for the globalization of Chinese enterprises, this CCG publication pays special attention to the BRI.

Overall, the trend of Chinese enterprises "going global" is irreversible and will continue to grow. This expansion is not only limited to the BRI framework, but also draws from past experience. Moving forward, Chinese enterprises should seek their own global development path. By adhering to the path of Reform and Opening-Up and WTO regulations, further integrating China into the world economy, Chinese enterprises can flourish in the global market. In the meantime, these enterprises can function as representatives of the success of China's Reform and Opening-up, sharing the benefits of China's development with the world. Guided by the hopeful prospects of Chinese enterprises and economic globalization, this book analyzes the achievements and challenges for globalizing Chinese enterprises. We hope it is of benefit to our readers.

June 2019

Yongtu Long
Former Vice Minister of the Ministry
of Foreign Trade and Economic Cooperation
and Former Secretary-General
of the Boao Forum for Asia
Beijing, China

Foreword by Dewang Cao

Chinese Enterprises in the New Context of Economic Globalization

Globalization entered a phase of rapid development at the end of the 1980s and the beginning of the 1990s, which had a far-reaching impact on the world economy. This was supported by uninhibited flows of technology, goods, capital, information and talent around the world, improving the efficiency of resource allocation and boosting global growth. Throughout this process, China took an active role in economic globalization. Especially after joining the WTO, China has become an important participant, beneficiary and contributor to globalization.

Against this backdrop, China's OFDI has risen from almost zero to one of the highest in the world. Since the "go global" strategy was proposed in March 2000 during the Third Session of the Ninth National People's Congress, Chinese enterprises' OFDI has grown quickly. High levels of growth continued into the twenty-first century, with Chinese enterprises' OFDI entering a "golden" period. In 2015, China ranked second in the world for total OFDI flows. According to the Ministry of Commerce, after 14 years of rapid growth, that year Chinese FDI hit a record amount of US$ 196.15 billion, with a year-on-year increase of 34.7%.

The development of an enterprise cannot be separated from its global footprint. When enterprises reach a certain stage of development, globalization is not only necessary for them to complete industrial transformation and upgrading, but it is also crucial to effective global allocation of resources. In today's context of globalization, it is impossible for enterprises' business activities to be contained to just a single country, place or market. Rather, it is necessary to look globally to seek more markets, resources and technology. Fuyao Glass Industry Group was one of the very first Chinese manufacturers to go global. In 1994, it began its overseas expansion by establishing Greenville Glass in the US, selling automobile glass across North America. Twenty years later, after gaining sufficient overseas experience, Fuyao started large-scale investment and set up factories in Dayton, Ohio and Mt. Zion, Illinois. Rather than switching to real estate or finance, Fuyao remained focused on its core glass business, investing in markets from Russia to the US.

However, in recent years, the willingness of some countries to promote globalization has weakened. Anti-globalization and approaches such as unilateralism and protectionism have grown stronger, with various "anti-globalization" measures emerging. With anti-globalization sentiments rising, there is a growing tendency towards investment protectionism. Many countries have implemented security reviews and antitrust policies. Some countries use disguised means to target multinational companies, such as using laws and administrative measures such as environmental regulations. There is also increasing use of national security provisions and antitrust lawsuits to restrict the inflow of foreign capital. For instance, the Committee on Foreign Investment in the United States (CFIUS) has adopted more complex regulatory practices, thereby becoming a barrier for foreign investors.

According to UNCTAD's *World Investment Report*, global FDI decreased by 23% in 2017. The main reason for this was a 29% reduction in super-large-scale mergers and acquisitions and corporate restructuring, among which, FDI inflow to the US decreased by 40% to US$ 275 billion.

Meanwhile, while Chinese OFDI grew over the past few years, certain problems were revealed too. Investment in non-core fields grew steadily and there was a rush to invest in sectors such as real estate, hospitality industry, entertainment and sports clubs, requiring sizeable investment and the taking on of large amounts of debt. This irrational, high-risk and debt-fueled investment attracted significant government and public attention. Recently, with more scrutiny on this kind of unreasonable investment, many have adjusted their behavior. In the first half of 2018, the Ministry of Commerce data clearly shows that most Chinese enterprises' outbound investment flowed into renting, business services, manufacturing, mining, retail and wholesale. Meanwhile, there were no new major investments in the real estate, sports or entertainment sectors.

Current trends in Sino-US trade relations not only affect globalization but also deeply impact Chinese enterprises investing in America. As trade tensions escalate, this year, the US has announced several rounds of tariffs on Chinese products, as well as stepping up its supervision on foreign capital. Recently, US President Donald Trump signed the National Defense Authorization Act, which strengthens the power of CFIUS, demanding that it more strictly scrutinize foreign acquisition of American companies, providing a national security assessment report for each case of foreign investment in a US company. In the future, Chinese investment in the US will be subject to greater uncertainty and regulation. Therefore, it is important for Chinese globalizing enterprises to improve their ability to control risks and pay strict attention to operational management, ensuring these are all in accordance with local laws and regulations.

The importance of compliance in the process of globalization of Chinese enterprises is becoming increasingly prominent. With the strengthening of supervision by governments and international organizations, as well as the threat of unilateralism and protectionism, compliance has become the main risk in the global operation of enterprises. If this risk cannot be managed, it will be a major obstacle to Chinese enterprises going global. Without compliance, even Chinese enterprises that have already expanded overseas will be hard-pressed to develop further. In recent years, in the process of enterprises' globalization, there have been frequent cases of enterprises breaking local regulations and laws. Even large, well-known multinational companies have been caught engaging in bribery in China. Similarly, Chinese enterprises overseas have also encountered difficulties in complying with local laws and regulations. Chinese enterprises must put compliance front and center of their globalization strategy; it is the only way for these enterprises to achieve sustainable overseas development, especially in the light of new and changing laws and regulations. Compliance as an attitude should be embedded into enterprises' working culture and realized through the creation of a dedicated compliance department and a rigorously enforced compliance management system.

Over the past decade, economic globalization has made huge contributions to the world's economic development, becoming an irreversible trend for future growth. However, globalization also faces new problems. It is increasingly obvious that global governance mechanisms need to be adjusted, improved and rebuilt. During these uncertain times for economic globalization, China has become a supporter, creator and leader of a new round of globalization. In global governance, China advocates an open, inclusive and balanced approach, pursuing a more just and win-win approach. In international trade, China supports the multilateral trade system and continues to open up its market. China has implemented a series of opening-up policies that lower the bar for market entry and creates a more attractive market with better protection of intellectual and property rights.

China's BRI will also provide more opportunities and a wider scope for Chinese enterprises to go global. Chinese outbound enterprises have the potential to lead a new round of globalization and further contribute to the construction of a community with a shared future for mankind.

August 2019

Dewang Cao
Chairman, Fuyao Glass Industry Group Co., Ltd.,
Founder and Donor, Heren Charitable Foundation
Beijing, China

Preface to the Globalization of Chinese Enterprises Series

While the global economy has begun to recover in recent years, rising protectionism and anti-globalization sentiment have led to a decline of global foreign direct investment (FDI). The *World Investment Report*, released by the United Nations Conference on Trade and Development (UNCTAD) in January 2019, shows that in 2018, global FDI fell by 19% to US$ 1.2 trillion, the lowest point since the financial crisis. It was also the third consecutive annual drop in global FDI. FDI inflows to developed countries fell by 40% to US$ 451 billion, the lowest level since 2004, and European inflows suffered a drastic 73% drop. Under the shadow of rising protectionism, global FDI growth and the global economic recovery are hampered by growing investment risks and geopolitical risks such as Sino-US trade frictions. In *Global Economic Prospects* issued in June 2019, the World Bank downgraded its global economic outlook for the next 2 years, warning that the global economy faces significant downside risks and is vulnerable to trade tensions and financial turmoil.

Over the past 40 years of Reform and Opening-up, China has moved on from its initial limited understanding and conservative response to globalization. It has gradually become a new power that accepts and promotes globalization, with a major impact on the world. Since China joined the World Trade Organization (WTO) at the beginning of the twenty-first century, Chinese enterprises have fully integrated into the world economy. They have increasing opportunities to be part of and to understand international markets, allowing them to better learn and absorb advanced technology, operation and management methods from foreign enterprises. In 2013, China's outbound FDI (OFDI) broke the US$ 100 billion mark for the first time. In 2014, for the first time, China's inbound and outbound capital flows came close to equilibrium. If third-country financing and reinvestment are included, China had already become a net capital exporter in that year. In 2016,[1] China's OFDI reached an all-time high of US$ 196.15 billion, a year-on-year increase of 34.7%.

[1]2016 Statistical Bulletin on China's Foreign Direct Investment, jointly issued by The Ministry of Commerce, the National Bureau of Statistics, and the State Administration of Foreign Exchange.

Despite its economic miracle, China remains susceptible to the same ups and downs that the rest of the global economy experiences. Today, as globalization encounters difficulties and challenges, China persists in opening up to the world and strives to offer fairer and more inclusive options for economic globalization through the Belt and Road Initiative (BRI). The BRI also provides a new impetus for the recovery of the global economy. By the end of 2018, China had signed 170 intergovernmental cooperation agreements with a total of 122 countries and 29 international organizations. The total import-export volume between China and countries along the Belt and Road has reached US$ 6.47 trillion, creating 244,000 local jobs and nearly US$ 500 billion in newly signed external contracts. In addition, China has built 82 overseas economic and trade cooperation zones along the Belt and Road and its FDI into BRI countries has reached US$ 80 billion from 2013 to 2018.[2]

In today's globalized world, companies cannot truly succeed while staying cozy at home in their own domestic or regional markets. Globalized resource allocation and global expansion of business have become key to the prospects of any major enterprise.

As a latecomer to emerging markets, what are the current foreign investment trends and new features of globalizing Chinese enterprises? What difficulties and challenges do they face in the new context of globalization? How can they survive and thrive overseas? And how can they make progress in climbing the global economic value chain? We believe the answers to such questions are of great reference value and significance to enterprises in all countries in the contemporary context of globalization.

As a think tank dedicated to the research of globalizing enterprises, the Center for China and Globalization (CCG) pursues long-term, in-depth study, bringing together the insights of scholars, entrepreneurs and government officials to make research contributions to the "going out" of Chinese enterprises and to support their overseas development.

CCG launched China's only "blue book" on the globalization of Chinese enterprises, the *Report on Chinese Enterprises Globalization*, an annual book published since 2014. This publication summarizes successful experiences of globalizing Chinese enterprises from multiple perspectives, probing their operating environment, the problems and risks they face, and proposing corresponding policies and countermeasures. The report provides a valuable reference for Chinese enterprises to help optimize foreign investment strategy and better grasp the opportunities and challenges they face in the process of globalization.

Since 2014, CCG's annual China Outbound Forum has developed into a unique global platform for discussion on China's development and go-global process. The forum features hundreds of leading experts from domestic and foreign governments, business circles and academia. It has become the most representative and authoritative high-end forum on the theme of the internationalization of Chinese enterprises. CCG has also published a number of English books, such as *China*

[2]https://www.yidaiyilu.gov.cn/.

Goes Global: How China's Overseas Investment is Transforming Its Business Enterprises, Handbook on China and Globalization, and *China's Domestic and International Migration Development*. These works present the fruits of CCG's ongoing research into the globalization of enterprises and talent.

This latest series of CCG English publications on this theme draws together and synthesizes the experiences of globalizing Chinese enterprises. It also highlights the initiative of Chinese entrepreneurs and provides other countries with useful lessons from the internationalization from Chinese enterprises.

The successful publication of the "Globalization of Chinese Enterprises" was only possible with support from various quarters. Firstly, we would like to thank CCG Chairmen Chen Deming, Long Yongtu, Chen Qizong and He Yafei for their guidance, and Heren Charitable Foundation for their strong support. We also greatly appreciate expert input from CCG's Academic Expert Committee and the hard work of CCG researchers. In addition, we would like to express sincere gratitude to Springer for their support. We hope that this series will play a role in promoting the globalization of Chinese enterprises, helping the rest of the world deepen their understanding of Chinese enterprises, and help share with others the valuable experiences of globalizing Chinese enterprises.

December 2019

Dr. Huiyao Wang
President of CCG
Beijing, China

Dr. Lu Miao
Secretary General of CCG
Beijing, China

Contents

About the Authors

Dr. Huiyao Wang is the Founder and President of Center for China and Globalization (CCG), the leading Chinese non-government think tank. Dr. Wang is also the Vice Chairman of China Association for International Economic Cooperation Association of the Ministry of Commerce, and Chairman of China global Talent Society under the Ministry of Human Resources and Social Security. In addition, he is the Dean of Institute of Development Studies of China Southwestern University of Finance and Economics and a Vice Chairman of China Western (Overseas) Returned Scholars Association. Dr. Wang sits on the Migration Advisory Board of International Organization of Migration (IOM) of United Nation. He is also a member of Yale University Asia Development Advisory Council, Advisory Board of Ivey Business School in Asia and Duke Kunshan University Advisory Board.

Dr. Wang pursued his Ph.D. studies in international business and global management at University of Western Ontario and University of Manchester. He was a Senior Fellow at Harvard Kennedy School and a Visiting Fellow at Brookings Institution as well as a Senior Fellow at Asia Pacific Foundation of Canada. He has taught at Peking University, Tsinghua University and University of Western Ontario as adjunct professor. He has also authored and edited over 70 books and more than 100 articles and papers in both Chinese and English on global trade, global governance, global migration, China outbound and inbound investment, Chinese Diasporas and Chinese think tanks. His latest English books include Handbook on China and Globalization (Edward Elgar Publishing, 2019); China's Domestic and International Migration Development (Springer, 2019); China Goes Global: How China's Overseas Investment is Transforming Its Business Enterprises (Palgrave Macmillan, 2016).

Dr. Lu Miao is the Co-founder, and Secretary-General of the Center for China and Globalization (CCG), a Beijing-based non-governmental Chinese think tank, which has been recognized as one of the world's top 100 and china's best independent think tank. Through her vision and unwavering dedication, she helped build a strong foundation for the organization's research and policy advisory capacities over areas of international migration, global trade and investment relations, and global governance. Dr. Miao serves as the Deputy-Secretary General at the Writing Center of Beijing Normal University. In addition, She was the Young Leader of 2020 Munich Security Conference (MSC).

Dr. Miao is an experienced public speaker, having delivered keynote speeches, participated and moderated numerous panels at home and abroad, like Doha Forum and Astana Club Meeting. As an accomplished scholar, she has 30 publications in Chinese and English with top publishers including the Chinese Academy of Social Sciences Press, Springer, Edward Edgar, and Palgrave Macmillan. Dr. Miao holds a Ph.D. degree in Contemporary Chinese Studies from the Beijing Normal University and was a visiting fellow at New York University and Harvard University. She is also a Lien Fellow with Lien Ying Chow Legacy Fellowship at Singapore Nanyang Technological University and a new member of the Hupan University, an exclusive top elite program founded by Alibaba's Jack Ma that admits only the most outstanding social and business entrepreneurs under 35. Dr. Miao was a post-doctor at the Beijing Normal University and Hong kong of Science and Technology.

List of Figures

List of Tables

Chapter 1
Current Trends and Features of Outbound Investment Worldwide

1.1 Outline

With the deepening of economic globalization, the internationalization of Chinese enterprises has also seen rapid development. This is especially true in the 21st century, the golden age of the "go global" strategy for Chinese companies. Despite the financial crisis of 2008 and 2009 and weak outbound investment worldwide, China's OFDI flows have seen significant gains, growing ever more diverse in terms of investment destinations, industries and investment methods. However, the aftermath of the global financial crisis and the growing trend of anti-globalization in western countries has created new challenges for the globalization of Chinese enterprises.

The Center for China and Globalization (CCG), an observer, researcher and supporter of China's "go global" strategy, has consistently focused on the trajectory of globalizing Chinese enterprises, analyzing the relevant context of current events, international politics, economic and environmental issues. Through such research, CCG aims to decode existing patterns and map out the future direction of globalizing Chinese enterprises. This analysis helps CCG provide strategic, far-sighted recommendations to overcome the challenges Chinese enterprises face in the process of globalization. This work is a useful reference for enterprises, governments, and other research institutes. Moreover, CCG offers an open, inclusive and cooperative platform, as a think tank serving as a connecting point between research and recipient, providing intellectual support for the globalization of Chinese enterprises.

This book, published by CCG, presents nearly 3000 data samples on the outbound investment of Chinese firms. Both quantitative and qualitative research methods are used to analyze the features of Chinese enterprises' globalization. This analysis provides a reliable reference for enterprises that have already gone global and those that plan to. In particular, this book investigates challenges confronted by Chinese companies when doing business in foreign countries. It summarizes research covering three angles, namely: the current situation, causation analysis and corresponding

H. Wang and L. Miao, *The Globalization of Chinese Enterprises: Trends and Characteristics*, The Chinese Enterprise Globalization Series,
https://doi.org/10.1007/978-981-15-4646-4_1

solutions, and recommendations for firms, government departments and other institutions. This book mainly focuses on the globalization of Chinese enterprises from 2014 to 2017.

In the 21st century, globalizing Chinese enterprises witnessed rapid development with increasing levels of outbound investment. However, in 2017, Chinese OFDI experienced a decrease. From the end of 2016, the Chinese government increased its control over the risk management of outbound investment by strengthening regulations on the authenticity and compliance of Chinese firms' outbound investment. As a result, the OFDI of Chinese enterprises gradually cooled down and adopted a more rational pattern. As investment growth declined, the investment structure was able to further develop and mature.

In 2017, China's OFDI flows showed negative growth for the first time since China began releasing annual statistics in 2003. The annual total of $158.29 billion was down 19.3% from 2016. Nevertheless, Chinese outbound investment continues to becoming increasingly influential around the world, accounting for more than 10% of total investment worldwide for two consecutive years. At the same time, China's outbound investment has exceeded inbound investment three years in a row. By the end of the 2017, China's total outbound investment amounted to $1.8 trillion, accounting for 5.9% of the global total and ranking China the second in the world.

2017 saw both the global economy and global trade grow at the fastest rate since 2011, with growth of 3% and 4.7% respectively. By contrast, outbound investment decreased worldwide in 2016 and 2017. For instance, in 2017, cross-border mergers and acquisitions (M&A) and announced greenfield investments decreased by 22% and 14% respectively. In addition, levels of investment in developed countries shifted drastically while levels of investment in developing countries remained stable and robust. Generally speaking, international investment policies are becoming more liberalized and supportive, but protectionist measures adopted by certain countries remain a cause for concern.

1.2 The Current Situation and Features of Outbound Investment Worldwide

Since the financial crisis, the word economy has entered a period of slow recovery. However, influenced by trade frictions, financial turmoil, geopolitical tension and other factors, the global economic recovery has weakened, with the growth rate falling to 2.3% in 2019, according to the United Nation World Economic Situation and Prospects Report. Covid-19 has dealt a further blow to global economy, which may face the greatest challenge in nearly a century.

2017 IMF data shows that the GDP growth of developed countries was 2.2%, a 0.5% point increase from 2016. The US, the Euro Zone and Japan were the primary drivers behind the growth in developed countries. GDP growth for emerging markets and developing countries was 4.6%, with Russia and Brazil helping to overturn the trend of negative growth. In 2017, global commodity trading welcomed the fastest growth since 2011, up 4.7%. Nonetheless, given the trends of anti-globalization and trade protectionism, the world economy still faces many challenges.

In 2017, the amount of FDI decreased drastically by 23%, totaling $1430 billion. Geographically, America remains the largest outbound investor, while Japan replaced China to be the second largest investor, with China slipping down to third place. From a sectoral perspective, cross-border transaction decreased across the board. The mining industry suffered the largest drop, while manufacturing and service industries remained subdued. Regarding modes of investment, FDI was primarily comprised of M&As, supplemented by greenfield investment. However, both types of investment saw an overall downturn in 2017. Consequently, the growth of global value chains also slowed.

1.2.1 The Largest Drop in Global FDI Levels in Recent Years

Since 2014, the global economy has been in a steady state of recovery. However, from 2014 to 2017, FDI saw a downward trend, except for a significant increase in 2015. In 2014, many factors led to a decrease in global FDI flows, including the US draw down of quantitative easing, geopolitical crises in Eastern Europe and the Middle East, and the imbalanced recovery of the Euro Zone. After a one-year increase in 2015, the dominant causes of decreasing FDI over 2016 and 2017 appear to be the slow recovery of global markets and the rise of anti-globalization and protectionist policies and measures. Not only did FDI continue to fall in this period, the FDI drop in 2017 was also more severe compared to 2016.

The rising tide of anti-globalization worldwide appears to be the main culprit for the drop of global FDI in 2017. In the US, the Trump administration implemented unilateral and protectionist policies that increased tariffs on international trade. In Europe, elections in certain countries reflected a right-wing shift, hindering the progress of globalization. Furthermore, some European and North American countries strengthened their supervision and set up approval mechanisms for FDI. These crucial trends stood out as the major elements behind the continued shrinking of global FDI (Fig. 1.1).[1]

1.2.2 FDI Flows to Developed Economies Fluctuated but Flows to Developing Economies Remained Stable

From 2014 to 2017, global investment into developing countries remained stable, totaling around US $700 billion. Investment to developed countries experienced a period of volatility. After the 91.3% increase in global FDI in 2015, there followed

[1]UNCTAD (2018).

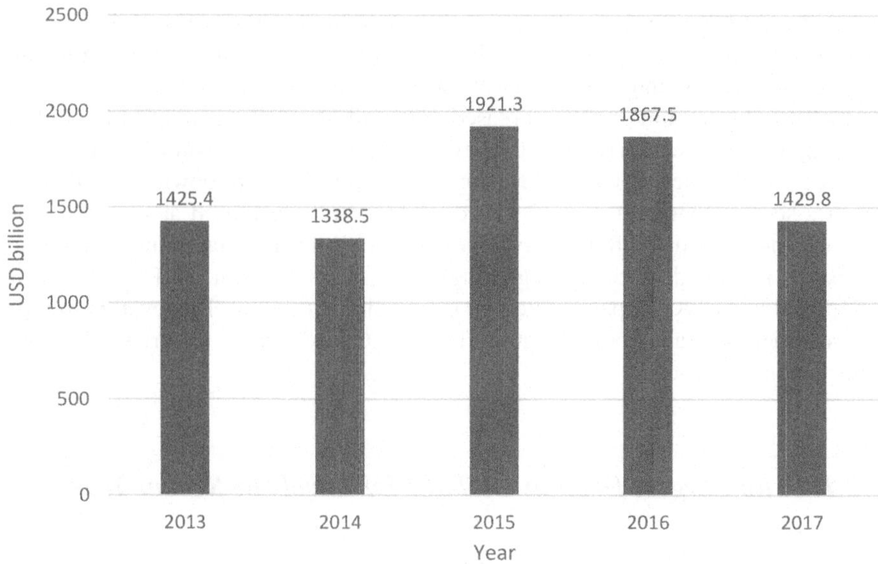

Fig. 1.1 Global FDI inflows, 2013–2017. *Source* UNCTAD <World Investment Report 2018>

a 37.1% decrease in 2017. Developing countries in Asia continued being a popular destination for international investors, and therefore did not feel the negative effects of the global economic slowdown as much as other regions. This was especially true for East, Southeast and South Asia, which saw rapid growth in international investment.

In 2017, the amount of global investment inflows to developed countries was $712.4 billion, accounting for 49.8% of the total investment worldwide. FDI to developing countries came to $670.7 billion, making up 46.9% of total global investment. The remaining 3.3% went to transition economies, a total of $46.8 billion.

Causal analysis shows that developed economies in North America and Europe suffered from slow economic recovery and implemented stricter supervision of foreign investment over this period, which led to a sharp decline in investment inflows. In contrast, the steady growth of global FDI inflows into Asian countries can be attributed to the relatively stable political situation, large market potential, and the strong development of the digital economy (Fig. 1.2).

1.2.3 Cross-Border M&A and Greenfield Investment

Both cross-border M&A and greenfield investment have fluctuated in recent years. After hitting a high point in 2016, both modes of investment saw decreases in 2017. Meanwhile, in 2017, cross-border M&A and greenfield investment amounts converged.

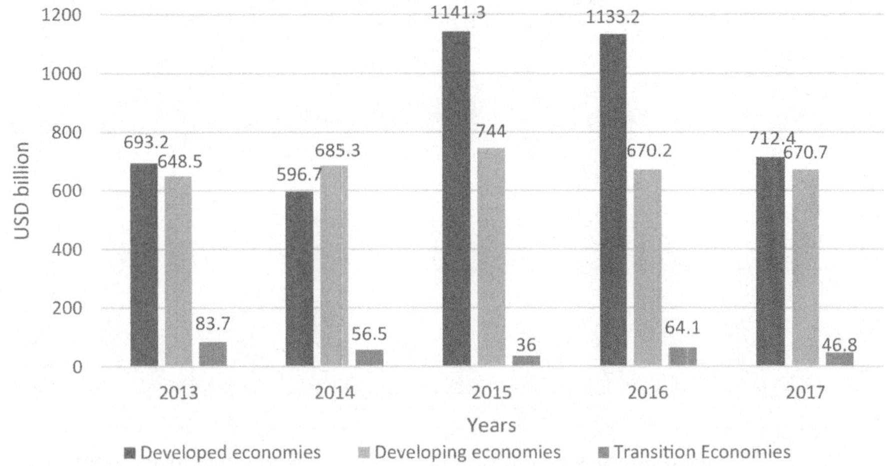

Fig. 1.2 Comparisons of FDI to different types of economy, 2013–2017. *Source* UNCTAD <World Investment Report 2018>

In 2017, cross-border M&A witnessed a dramatic drop of 21.8% to US$694 billion. Despite the fact that the total amount of capital involved in cross-border M&As decreased, the number of M&As actually saw a small 5% increase to 6,967 cases. This shows that in 2017, large-scale M&As decreased in comparison with 2016. M&A activity did not only cool in manufacturing and services. M&As in the primary sector also shrank severely by 70%. However, other sectors saw large gains; there was a 43% increase in M&As in business services, 63% in machinery and equipment and 66% in information and communication.

Similarly, in 2017, greenfield investment decreased 13.6% to US $720 billion. Of note, the total amount of greenfield investment in manufacturing was $338 billion, a 14% increase compared with the previous year. Nevertheless, greenfield investment into primary industry and service industry both saw reductions of 61% and 25% respectively. The decrease varied across sectors, ranging from 51% in construction to 26% in electricity, gas and water as well as transport, storage and communications (Fig. 1.3).

1.2.4 International Policy Trends Toward Liberalization and Investment Facilitation

From 2008 to 2017, an increasing number of countries enacted policies regarding international investment. In 2017, 65 countries and economies launched a total of over 126 policy measures affecting foreign investment. This represented the highest number of countries implementing investment measures and the highest total number of policy measures in a decade, up by 25 and 58 respectively since 2008. Of these

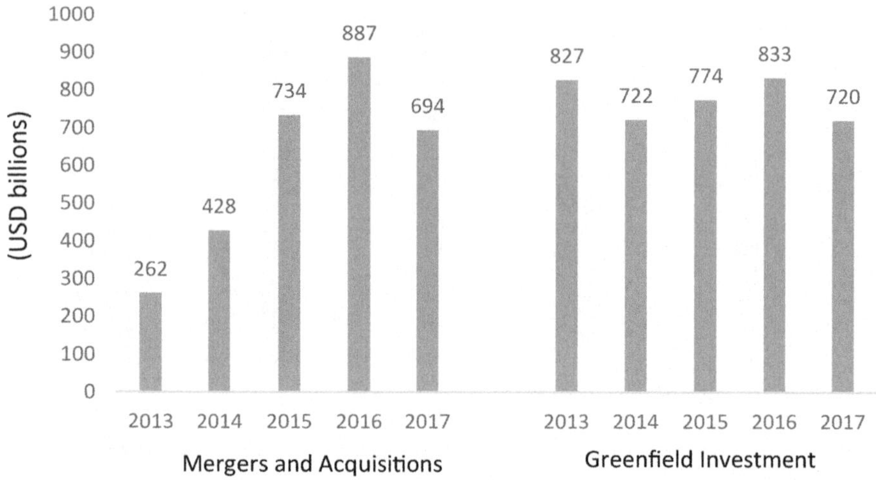

Fig. 1.3 Comparisons of FDI by different investment modes. *Source* UNCTAD <World Investment Report 2018>

policies, 93 were related to investment liberalization and investment promotion, while 18 were aimed at restriction and regulation (Table 1.1).

The specific characteristics of new investment varied by year. In 2014, some countries focused on loosening control over the ownership of foreign capital and opening up new sectors to foreign investors. For instance, India loosened restrictions on foreign investment in railway construction, while Indonesia increased foreign investment caps to 85% in medicine, risk investment and electricity generation. In 2015, emerging markets in Asia made particular efforts to facilitate and liberalize investment. For example, when Prime Minister Modi assumed office, India moved to allow 100% direct foreign investment in civil aviation and lowered the entry threshold for international airlines to enter India's aviation market. In addition, India passed measures allowing foreign companies to hold up to a 74% share in mature medicine programs even without prior government approval, and for foreign investors to hold 100% of new pharmaceutical enterprises. In 2016, despite the trend of global investment policies moving toward liberalization and facilitation, some developed countries were tightening foreign investment regulations and increasing supervision and restrictions on foreign investment.

In 2017, emerging Asian powers continued expanding policies to attract foreign investment. China lifted 30 restrictions on foreign investment into the Chinese market, ranging from services to manufacturing and mining. Laos abolished the requirement to register the lowest standard for foreign investment. Myanmar gave far more leeway to\ foreign investors to hold shares in domestic companies. Conversely, certain developed economies continued to strengthen barriers to foreign investment. Japan revised its foreign investment audit system. The cabinet of Germany passed further amendments to the Foreign Economic Law. The United Kingdom proposed

Table 1.1 Changes in the number of foreign investment policies

	2008	2009	2010	2011	2012	2013	2014	2015	2016	2017
Number of countries presenting regulations	40	46	54	51	57	60	41	49	59	65
Total number of policies changed	68	89	116	86	92	87	74	100	125	126
Liberalization and facilitation policies	51	61	77	62	65	63	52	75	84	93
Restrictive policies	15	24	33	21	21	21	12	14	22	18
Neutral policies	2	4	6	3	6	3	10	11	19	15

Source UNCTAD <<World Investment Report 2018>>

measures to strengthen the review and investigation mechanisms on foreign M&As of British enterprises.

These trends make clear that more countries are paying closer attention to foreign investment. Most aim to create a more amiable environment for FDI. However, a number of countries have decided to adopt a more cautious attitude towards FDI. Notably, it tends to be developed countries that have introduced restrictive regulations regarding foreign investment. In general, these countries have stepped up review mechanisms for foreign M&A, especially for strategic assets and high-tech enterprises. Moreover, the formulation of International Investment Agreements (IIAs) also witnessed a turning point; 2017 saw the lowest amount of IIAs signed since 1983. Moreover, for the first time in history, the number of agreements that were terminated exceeded the number of new agreements signed. By contrast, negotiations on large-scale regional agreements have maintained good momentum, especially in Asia and Africa.

Reference

UNCTAD, *World Investment Report 2018.*

Chapter 2
Current Trends and Features of China's OFDI

Despite rising trade barriers and the trend of anti-globalization, China's economy continues to grow and develop. According to the National Bureau of Statistics, in 2017, China's GDP broke the CNY 80 trillion mark for the first time, reaching CNY 82.7 trillion. The growth rate of 6.9% was higher than 2016, the first increase in seven years.[1] Although Chinese enterprises' OFDI slowed, investment fields and patterns stabilized. At the same time, investments diversified and broadened in scope, with particular success along the Belt and Road.

2.1 China's OFDI Decreases for the First Time as Policies Rationalize the Go-Global Movement

2017 saw the first decline in China's OFDI since China began releasing annual statistics in 2003. China's OFDI in 2017 amounted to US$ 158.29 billion, a decrease of 19.3% compared to the previous year. Nevertheless, it was still China's second-largest OFDI total in history, second only to 2016, meaning that China accounted for more than 10% of the global FDI total for two consecutive years. In terms of investment flows, China slipped from the second to third, after the US (US$342.27 billion) and Japan (US$160.45 billion). In terms of two-way investment flows, China's OFDI has exceeded inward FDI for three consecutive years.[2]

After more than a decade of rapid growth, by 2017, China's OFDI was 58.6 times the level in 2002. In that time, China's OFDI global ranking has risen from 26th in 2002, to the second in 2015, and then third in 2017. In the five years from 2013 to 2017, China's accumulative FDI amounted to US$731.07 billion—equal to over 40% of China's total past FDI. These figures show the rapid development that occurred during these years (Fig. 2.1).

[1]National Bureau of Statistics of China.

[2]Ministry of Commerce of the People's Republic of China.

H. Wang and L. Miao, *The Globalization of Chinese Enterprises: Trends and Characteristics*, The Chinese Enterprise Globalization Series,
https://doi.org/10.1007/978-981-15-4646-4_2

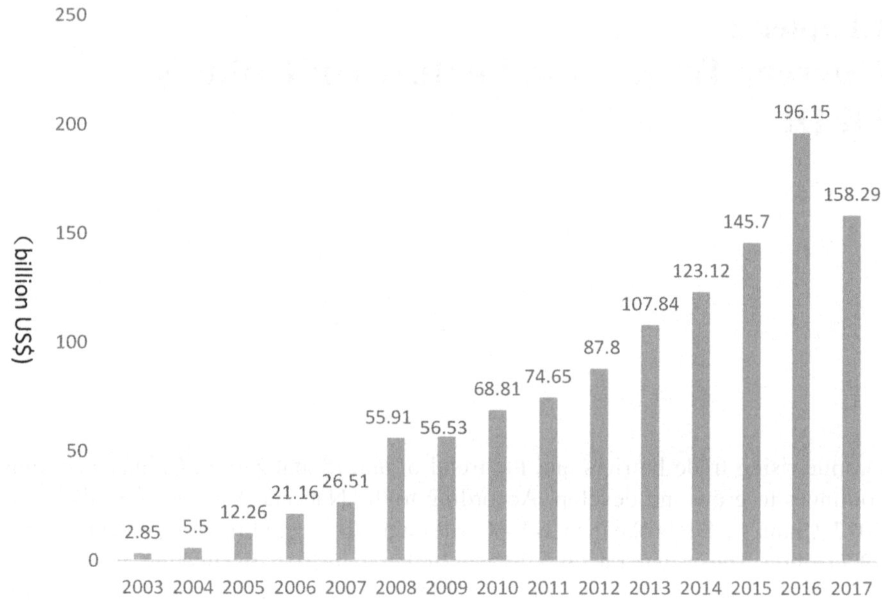

Fig. 2.1 China's OFDI from 2003 to 2017. *Source* Figure created by CCG with data from the Ministry of Commerce of the PRC, National Bureau of Statistics PRC, and State Administration of Foreign Exchange, PRC

During this period, the Chinese government strengthened risk management for enterprises' overseas investments, implementing a series of policies to guide enterprises to invest lawfully and reduce risks. Following the strengthening of the "go global" strategy in 2016, the Chinese government enacted a number of policies related to enterprises' globalization, including "Guiding Opinions on Further Directing and Regulating the Direction of Overseas Investment" and "Circular on Promulgating the Regulations on Outbound Investment and Business Activities of Private Enterprises." As a part of this push, the National Development and Reform Commission enacted "Measures for the Administration of Overseas Investment of Enterprises" which helped streamline and decentralize administration of OFDI investment. In 2018, two other policies were enacted, namely, "Interim Measures for Filing (Approving) Reports of Outbound Investment" and "The Catalog for the Outbound Investment in Sensitive Industries." These policy changes had a clear impact on enterprises' outbound investment. In particular, the Chinese government's more refined approach to supervising outbound investment helped encourage a healthier, more sustainable mode and structure of outbound investment.

Table 2.1 Regional distribution of China's OFDI in 2017

Area	OFDI (US$ billion)	Year on year growth (%)	Percentage (%)
Europe	18.46	72.7	11.7
Africa	4.1	70.8	2.6
Oceania	5.11	−1.9	3.2
Asia	110.04	−15.5	69.5
Latin America	14.08	−48.3	8.9
North America	6.5	−68.1	4.1
Total	158.29	−19.3	100.0

Source Data from Ministry of Commerce of the PRC, National Bureau of Statistics of the PRC, State Administration of Foreign Exchange

2.2 OFDI Destinations Diversify, with Rapid Growth in Europe and Africa

Chinese OFDI spans a large number of countries and regions. By the end of 2017, 25,500 Chinese investors had invested abroad, starting 39,200 OFDI enterprises across 189 foreign countries, accounting for over 80% of countries worldwide.[3] At the end of 2017, the total capital of these firms spread over Asia, the Americas, Europe, Africa and Oceania amounted to US$6 trillion.

In terms of geographical distribution, Chinese firms have primarily invested in Asia and America, with investment in Europe and Africa growing quickly. By the end of 2017, the most popular destination for Chinese OFDI was Asian Markets such as Hong Kong, Singapore, Indonesia, Macau, Kazakhstan, Laos, Korea, Pakistan, Myanmar. The total investment in the region amounted to US$1.139 trillion, accounting for 63% of total OFDI. The second largest investment destination was America, totaling US$473.8 billion and accounting for 26.2% of the total. This is followed by Europe (US$110.86 billion, 6.1%), Africa (US$43.3 billion, 2.4%) and Oceania (US$41.76 billion 2.3%). In 2017, investment into Europe and Africa increased to US$18.46 billion, a 72.7% increase from the previous year (11.7% of 2017 total investment) and US$4.1 billion, a 70.8% increase from the previous year (2.6% of 2017 total investment), respectively (Table 2.1).

At the same time, investment into the Americas saw a dramatic decrease. In 2017, investment into the US and Canada was US$6.43 billion and US$0.32 billion, shrinking by 62.1% and 88.9%, respectively. Investment in Asia and Oceania saw reductions as well, of $110.04 billion and $5.11 billion, representing falls of 15.5% and 1.9% respectively (Fig. 2.2).

[3]Outward Foreign Direct Investment (OFDI) Enterprise: refers to an overseas enterprise in which the domestic investor directly owns or controls 10% or more of the equity, voting rights or other equivalent interests.

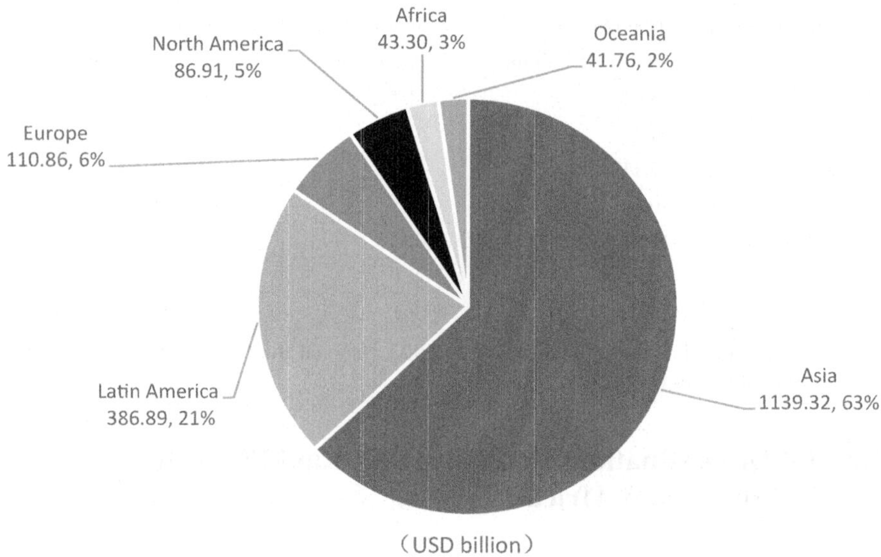

Fig. 2.2 Destinations of China's OFDI Stock (End of 2017). *Source* Data from Ministry of Commerce of the PRC, National Bureau of Statistics of the PRC, State Administration of Foreign Exchange

A large proportion of China's OFDI has flowed into developing economies. By the end of 2017, China's investment in developing economies came to US$1.552 trillion, accounting for 85.8% of total OFDI. Meanwhile, investment in developed and transitional economies accounted for 12.7% and 1.5% respectively. Investment by Chinese enterprises provides significant tax revenue to host countries and contributes to employment, creating a win-win situation for Chinese firms and host countries. In 2017, Chinese companies paid a variety of taxes to host countries totaling US$37.6 billion and hired 1.71 million local workers, an increase of 367,000 from the end of 2016.

2.3 China's OFDI Covers Many Sectors, with Particular Increases in Manufacturing, Wholesale and Retail, and Finance

Chinese firms have conducted outbound investment into all civilian sectors categorized in national statistics. Six sectors account for most of the total, namely, leasing and business services, wholesale and retail, information transmission/software and information technology, finance, mining and manufacturing. By the end of 2017, investment in leasing and business services came to US$615.77 billion, accounting for 34.1% of the total OFDI stock. This included investment activities with shareholding as the main purpose. Total investment in wholesale and retail amounted to US$226.43 billion, making up 12.5% of the total. Information transmission/software and information technology saw $218.9 billion of investment, 12.1% of the total. Investment in the financial sector made up 11.2% of the total, amounting to US$202.79 billion. 8.7% of total OFDI went into mining, coming to US$157.67 billion. Investment in manufacturing totaled US$140.3, 7.8% of the total, with investment in equipment manufacturing accounting for 45.8% of manufacturing investment.

In 2017, while China's OFDI decreased across many industries, investment in manufacturing, wholesale and retail, and finance continued to grow by 1.6%, 25.9% and 25.9%, respectively. Altogether, almost 80% of China's OFDI went to these three industries, together with leasing and business services.

With the optimization of investment structure in 2017 and reining in of irrational investment, investment in real estate and culture, sports and entertainment industries experienced sharp decreases of 55.1% and 93.3% respectively. This was in stark contrast to previous years, when OFDI into real estate jumped by 67.1% in 2014, 17.9% in 2015, and 95.8% in 2016 (Fig. 2.3).

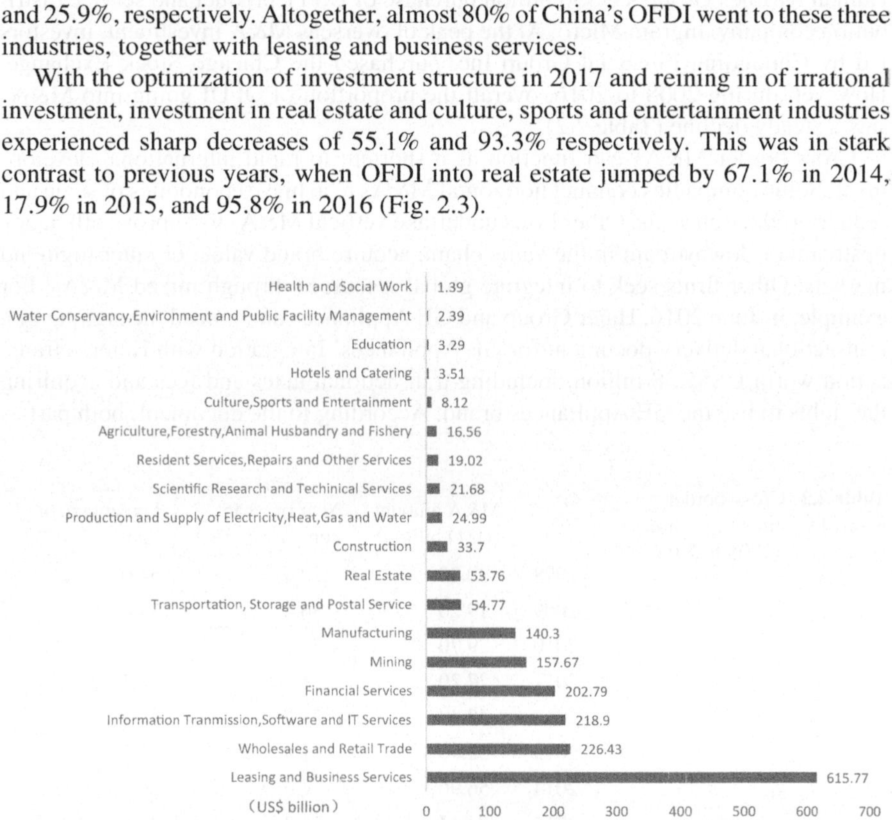

Fig. 2.3 Sectoral Distribution of China's OFDI Stock (End of 2017). *Source* Data from Ministry of Commerce of the PRC, National Bureau of Statistics of the PRC, State Administration of Foreign Exchange

2.4 Overseas M&As by Chinese Enterprises Grow but Fluctuate

In recent years, Chinese enterprises have been increasingly active in overseas mergers and acquisitions (M&As). In 2008, the year the financial crisis hit, Chinese companies' overseas M&A activity increased by 379.4%, with direct investment in M&As making up 54.0% of total OFDI that year. 2016 also saw high levels of overseas M&A activity for Chinese companies. Compared to the year before, in 2016, this type of investment increased by 148.6%, accounting for 44.1% of total OFDI that year. Notable deals that year included Haier Group's purchase of GE Appliances and Hainan Airlines Group's US$6 billion purchase of US IT product and service distribution company, Ingram Micro. At the peak of overseas M&A investment, investors led by Chongqing Financial Group Inc. purchased the Chicago Stock Exchange. However, during 2008 to 2016, overall the proportion of OFDI going into M&As saw a steady decline (Table 2.2).

Cross-border M&As can function as a shortcut to rapid international development. Some companies conduct horizontal M&As to achieve economies of scale and reduce production costs. Other firms undertake vertical M&As to improve efficiency upstream or downstream in the value chain, acquire brand value, or enter high-end markets. Other firms seek to integrate global resources through mixed M&As. For example, in June 2016, Haier Group and GE Appliances announced the signing of a transactional delivery document for GE Appliances' integration with Haier, a transaction worth US$5.58 billion, including transactional taxes and fees and acquiring the rights to use the GE Appliances brand. According to the document, both parties

Table 2.2 Cross-border M&A Investment by Chinese Enterprises (2008 to 2017)

Year	M&A amount (USD billion)	Year on year comparison (%)	Percentage of total (%)
2008	30.20	379.4	54.0
2009	19.20	−36.4	34.0
2010	29.70	54.7	43.2
2011	27.20	−8.4	36.4
2012	43.40	59.6	31.4
2013	52.90	21.9	31.3
2014	56.90	7.6	26.4
2015	54.44	−4.3	25.6
2016	135.33	148.6	44.1
2017	119.62	−11.6	21.1

Source Figure created by CCG with data from Ministry of Commerce of the PRC, National Bureau of Statistics of the PRC, State Administration of Foreign Exchange
Note M&A amount refers to FDI and foreign financing; Percentage refers to the proportion that M&A took of total OFDI

would cooperate worldwide, helping to improve both parties' competitiveness in fields such as industrial internet and medicine.

In 2017, although M&A activity decreased compared to the previous year, Chinese enterprises remained active in this area. In 2017, Chinese firms carried out 431 M&As worth a total of US$119.62 billion. This included US$33.47 billion of direct investment, accounting for 28% of total M&A transactions. It is worth noting that in 2017, Chinese companies engaging in overseas M&As greatly enlarged the scale of foreign financing, resulting in the largest overseas financing year for Chinese companies. This amounted to US$86.15 billion, an increase of around 70% compared with the previous year, with 72% of total M&A investment supported by foreign financing. One example of this was ChemChina's purchase of a 98.06% stake in Swiss company Syngenta for US$42.1 billion. This was the largest overseas M&A by a Chinese company since the implementation of the "go global" strategy and the second largest merger worldwide in 2017.

In terms of geographical scope, in 2017, outbound M&A investment by Chinese firms covered 56 countries and areas. The top 10 investment destinations were Switzerland, the US, Germany, Brazil, the UK, Indonesia, Hong Kong, Australia, the United Arab Emirates and Singapore.

Overseas M&As by Chinese firms covered a total of 18 industries, ranging from manufacturing and mining to the production and supply of utilities. M&As in manufacturing amounted to US$60.72 billion, involving 163 projects, doubling 2016 figures and ranking top in terms of M&A investment in 2017. Mining M&A investment amounted to US$11.41 billion, ranking second with an increase of 52.1%. The purchase of a 12% stake in Abu Dhabi National Oil Company (ADNOC) by China National Petroleum Corporation (CPNC) and Huaxin Group was the largest merger in this sector. Mergers in the production and supply of utilities amounted to US$12.65 billion, a 12.8% increase from the previous year and ranking third overall. The State Grid Corporation of China's purchase of CPFL in Brazil was the largest merger in this sector that year.

2.5 Participation in the BRI by Chinese Firms Benefitted Host Countries

During his visits to Kazakhstan and Indonesia in September and October 2013 respectively, Chinese President Xi Jinping first proposed building a "Silk Road Economic Belt" and a "21st Century Maritime Silk Road." On 14 and 15 May 2017, the first Belt and Road Forum for International Cooperation was held successfully in Beijing. During the summit, five policies were agreed on, covering policy coordination, infrastructure connection, trade facilitation, financial integration and people-to-people ties. A total of 76 large-scale projects and 270 subprojects were also announced.

Since the 1990s, globalization has seen rapid development. The world economy has become increasingly intertwined and world trade has maintained a growth rate higher than global production. At the same time, regional integration, as represented by the European Union, has also gradually advanced. However, the 2008 financial crisis severely impacted the global economy. The process of globalization began to stall, cross-border capital and trade flows fell to historic lows, and anti-globalization sentiment started to gain traction around the world.

These shifts saw many observers take a pessimistic view and wonder whether this was the "beginning of the end" for globalization. In contrast, others took the view that this was the beginning of a new phase of globalization. The BRI put forward by China aims to act as a platform for this new phase of globalization. Focusing on global governance and international cooperation, it is based on the principle of achieving shared growth through discussion and collaboration while pursuing win-win outcomes.

In the five years since it was launched, the BRI has been transformed from theory into action, with a series of solid achievements. Chinese enterprises have sought to actively participate in BRI projects and invested in countries along the Belt and Road. From 2013 to 2017, China invested US$80.73 billion in countries involved in the BRI and invested almost US$30 billion in more than 80 trade cooperation zones. Approximately 4,000 companies have set up in these zones, making these zones significant launch pads for local light industry, textile, building materials and family appliances, industries that have brought over 200,000 jobs to host countries (Fig. 2.4).

In 2017, there was a big increase in Chinese investment in countries along the BRI route across a wide range of sectors. According to China's Ministry of Commerce, in 2017, Chinese investors directly invested in 3,000 companies located in 57

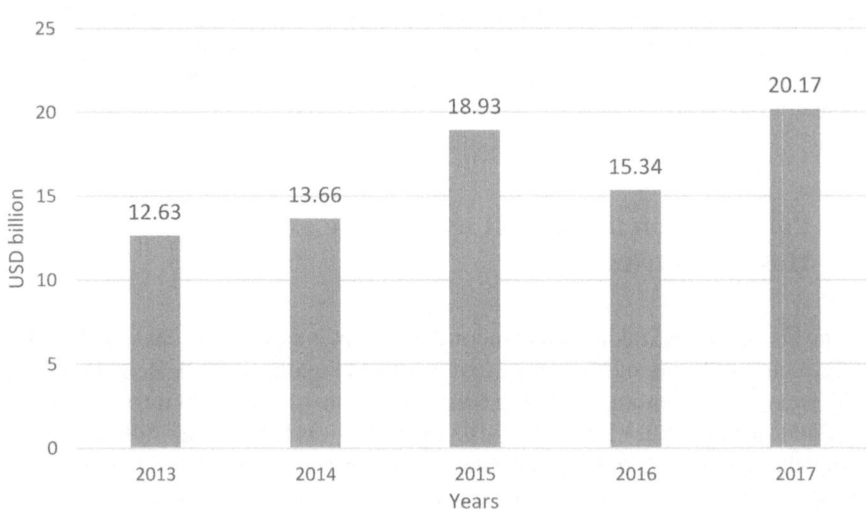

Fig. 2.4 China's Investment in Countries Along the Belt and Road. *Source* Figure created by CCG with data from the Ministry of Commerce of the PRC, National Bureau of Statistics of the PRC, State Administration of Foreign Exchange

countries along the BRI route. These investments covered 17 sectors and amounted to US$20.17 billion, an annual increase of 31.5%. Together, they accounted for 12.7% of China's total OFDI in 2017. The major BRI investment destinations were Singapore, Kazakhstan, Malaysia, Indonesia, Russia, Laos, Thailand, Vietnam, Pakistan and the United Arab Emirates. There were 76 cases of M&As between Chinese companies and companies along the BRI route, with total investment of US$16.28 billion, accounting for 13.6% of all overseas M&A activity. In particular, Indonesia, the United Arab Emirates, Singapore, India, Israel and Russia attracted over one billion dollars in M&A investment.

State-owned companies in the energy sector and infrastructure construction were the first cohort of Chinese enterprises that invested in countries along the BRI route, with both upstream and downstream private companies following in tow. On this basis, enterprises in the fields of science and technology and service industries have gradually become a new force making up the third cohort of Chinese enterprises operating along the BRI route. For example, the Chinese Enlightenment Clean Energy Group cooperated with local enterprises in Nairobi, Kenya to promote solar hot water system technology in affordable housing communities. For Kenya, a country that lacks electric power in places but abounds in solar resources, such technology not only helps to reduce electricity fees but also allows people to enjoy the benefits of hot running water. In Rwanda, set-top cable TV boxes produced by StarTimes Group and sold in the Rwandan market increased the number of TV channels available to local residents from one to over 40, which also resulted in a price reduction for these products.

Chapter 3
Problems Faced by Globalizing Chinese Enterprises and Proposed Solutions

As the "go global" movement accelerates, Chinese enterprises have encountered various problems in the process of globalization. These problems include insufficient ability to manage risks, such those stemming from law and politics; low levels of participation in the formulation of international standards; barriers to corporate brand internationalization strategy; and the limited internationalization of corporate talent. To help address these problems, this chapters maps out the current situation and challenges in each area, presents causal analysis, and proposes reasonable solutions accordingly.

3.1 Legal Risks

3.1.1 Current Situation: Enterprises "Going Global" Face High Legal Risk and Often Rely on Poor Local Legal Services

Legal risk refers to the risk of losses due to a company's business activities being non-compliant with legal requirements or losses caused by external legal events. It is the most significant form of risk for Chinese companies engaging in foreign investment, alongside political risk. According to CCG statistics, about 16% of terminations or losses regarding Chinese enterprises' foreign investment were directly or indirectly due to legal reasons. One-third of this was caused by improper access to the project due to non-compliance with laws of the host country. Another third was due to unfamiliarity with the labor laws of the host country.

At the same time, compared with countries such as the United Kingdom and the United States, Chinese law firms are significantly underdeveloped and on average have a low degree of internationalization. Therefore, Chinese law firms provide relatively weak legal services to Chinese enterprises investing abroad.

H. Wang and L. Miao, *The Globalization of Chinese Enterprises: Trends and Characteristics*, The Chinese Enterprise Globalization Series,
https://doi.org/10.1007/978-981-15-4646-4_3

The problems faced by companies in international dispute resolution are very complex. Experienced lawyers are required to handle issues ranging from the application of laws and choice of arbitration institutions to the choice of solutions and formulation of dispute resolution strategies. However, in general, the number of lawyers engaged in foreign-related legal business in Chinese law firms is seriously lacking. Most Chinese law firms focus on legal services which foreign lawyers are prohibited from engaging in in China or other areas of legal services related to doing business in China and traditional goods import and export. There is a lack of Chinese law firms providing quality legal services for Chinese enterprises investing overseas. According to the "Report on 'Going Global' of Chinese Enterprises from 2015 to 2016", 91% of respondents choose to employ local lawyers when international trade disputes arose.

3.1.2 Causal Analysis: Lack of Corporate Legal Awareness and Insufficient International Legal Talent

The level of legal knowledge and awareness surrounding Chinese companies "going global" remains insufficient. The first area in which awareness is lacking relates to use of legal services. Some Chinese companies investing abroad only get lawyers or legal personnel involved when signing a framework agreement. The notion of " action then law " (taking legal consultation after getting into trouble) leads Chinese enterprises building overseas investment teams to prioritize technical and business teams over legal teams. The lack of legal awareness and the unsystematic way of managing overseas investment obscures risk and can become a major reason for subsequent losses.

The second key factor regarding limited legal awareness is the tendency to ignore the standardization of negotiations and contract signing. In the process of cross-industry or off-line investments, some Chinese companies may be unfamiliar with the industry relevant to their overseas investment projects. This, coupled with the difficulty in coordinating teamwork from a pickup team on these investments, inevitably leads to key compliance issues being ignored in the process of negotiating and signing contracts. In addition, some Chinese companies make unrealistic verbal commitments in order to sign a cooperation agreement as soon as possible, thus setting themselves a potential trap and burying potential risks.

Thirdly, there is often a lack of prudent prior due diligence. In the process of "going global," some Chinese companies do not conduct in-depth preliminary due diligence on investment projects. This appears to be due to a lack of risk awareness and an over-eagerness to achieve rapid success in the endeavor. CCG survey results show that in the initial stage of selecting investment targets, about 70% of "go global" companies ignored the levels of local wages, tax policies, business dealings with local companies and other factors, all of which can have a negative impact down the line. The absence or inadequacy of due diligence not only brings risks to the company regarding the legality of the acquisition of assets and the risk of ownership, but also related to hidden debt or litigation risks of the purchased company. Even the legitimacy of the target company or asset itself can be difficult to guarantee without appropriate due diligence.

Lawyers and law firms that provide legal services to "go global" enterprises often face significant language barriers, as well as lack of diversity in staffing. First, Chinese lawyers face language barriers that prevent them from playing a prominent enough role in the "go global" process of Chinese companies, when language capabilities may be a prerequisite for engaging in international business. Many Chinese lawyers have good foundations in English or other foreign languages. However, for international commercial legal services, lawyers need to be able to use a foreign language to complete a large amount of written documentation and verbal communication in a short period of time. It is also necessary for lawyers to accurately understand what is expressed by the other party and make oral statements or defense in highly confrontational situations. Therefore, weak language capabilities can be an obstacle to success.

Moreover, local Chinese law firms had a relatively late start in development. There remains a serious shortage of international interdisciplinary legal talent. At present, the vast majority of employees of Chinese law firms are citizens of mainland China, with very few foreign or non-Chinese mainland employees. This results in a lack of diversity and insufficient internationalization of human resources, hindering the ability to provide international legal services. Consequently, many "go global" companies have received inadequate support from Chinese law firms.

3.1.3 Suggested Solutions

Enterprises need to take into account the issues above and consider the following proposed remedies.

Firstly, there is a need to raise legal awareness and attach more importance to the procurement of legal services. As professional legal experts working with or for a private company, lawyers can help companies avoid risk and help ensure compliance in production and operations. Lawyers can act as risk control personnel for enterprises, minimizing risk by participating in the drafting of transaction contracts between buyers and sellers. Legal personnel can also advise on the institutional operations of enterprises, clarifying the function of each department and organization, helping to improve an enterprise's operational efficiency. At the same time, employees of the company should receive regular training to enhance their legal awareness, ensuring the legal and compliance development of the company.

The second suggestion is for Chinese enterprises to conduct comprehensive and in-depth due diligence on prospective partners, projects or assets that are the focus of their investment and operations. At the same time, it is necessary to investigate the legal situation of the investment site in detail. Remaining unfamiliar with the investment enviorment in host countries may result in unpredictable risks and other issues over time.

Chinese law firms serving Chinese enterprises "going global" should, as a first priority, further internationalize their human resources. Law firms engaged in foreign-related legal business should be encouraged to attract high-quality foreign legal talent to join their firms. They should also support Chinese students studying abroad and legal professionals and specialists to practice in Chinese law firms. In addition, Hong Kong, Macao and Taiwan compatriots should be encouraged to study mainland law, take mainland legal professional qualification examinations and practice in mainland law firms. In short, it is necessary to improve the composition of staffing at Chinese law firms in various ways, improve their level of internationalization and international competitiveness, and let them play a greater role in the process of Chinese enterprises "go global."

Secondly, Chinese law firms should work to establish alliances with foreign organizations and deepen cooperation with international legal industry associations. In 2013, King & Wood Mallesons formed a global legal alliance with the UK law firm SJ Berwin, which greatly enhanced its strength and global influence. In addition, participating in international industry associations can aid in expanding cooperation and information sharing. In 1997, Jun He Law Firm took the lead in joining the leading international law firm associations LexMundi and Multilaw. Through this, they have built partnerships with some of the best law firms in major European and Asian countries. King & Wood Mallesons has joined the Pacific Rim Legal Advisers Alliance and the World Lawyers Alliance, while Dacheng Law Firm has joined the World Service Group. By joining the world's leading legal industry associations, Chinese firms can further expand the breadth and depth of their business, increasing their level of internationalization through a comprehensive platform that boasts the world's top law firms, accounting firms, investment companies, financial institutions and other professional service companies.

For legal industry associations, it is necessary to set up corresponding professional committees, organizing lawyers to conduct study exchanges and business training corresponding to international trade law. In addition, industry associations should actively organize exchanges between Chinese lawyers and foreign lawyers, selecting outstanding Chinese lawyers to study abroad to improve their understanding of foreign-related laws. It is also necessary to establish links and strengthen communication with foreign lawyers and local lawyers. At the same time, steps should be taken to develop the ability of Chinese law firms to "go global" along with Chinese companies.

For the Chinese government, it is essential to strengthen overseas investment legislation and develop intermediary legal services. First, the government should speed up the formulation of "The People's Republic of China Law on Overseas Investment Promotion," clarifying legal rights, obligations, business operations requirements, and supporting measures for overseas investment. To support the law, the "International Economic Cooperation Law", "Overseas Joint Venture Enterprise Law", "Overseas Investment Enterprise Income Tax Law", "Overseas Investment Management Regulations" and other relevant laws and regulations should be promulgated as soon as possible. The government should also establish an overseas investment legal system based on the "Law on Overseas Investment Promotion" along with corresponding regulations.

Secondly, the government should focus on developing intermediary services related to international legal business. This includes supporting the growth of intermediary services related to international legal business, such as professional consulting agencies, arbitrators, accreditation agencies and other intermediary services, especially those involved in international trade, maritime affairs, and international engineering. These institutions should seek to accelerate their internationalization process. At the same time, domestic lawyers, scholars, and related professionals need to be encouraged to serve as arbitrators in internationally renowned arbitration institutions such as the International Chamber of Commerce Arbitration and the Arbitration Institute of the Stockholm Chamber of Commerce.

3.2 Political Risk

3.2.1 Current Situation: Increasing Frequency of Geopolitical Incidents and Damage to Overseas Corporate Interests

Political risks pertaining to overseas investment are unpredictable and can have a range of impacts. The main source of political risk is instability of politics, policy and foreign currency exchange in host countries. In addition to market factors, political risk is a major factor that can hinder operational performance and cause international projects to fail. These risks include a sudden change of a host country's political system or regime, government collapses, wars, civil unrest, riots, revolutions, and policy changes that cause foreign companies to suffer losses.

Political risk is a crucial factor affecting Chinese companies' overseas investment. In 2001, more than 50 large-scale projects invested in by Chinese companies in Libya were halted to the outbreak of war, resulting in huge losses. After the war in Libya in 2011, all Chinese-funded projects were left stranded. Other projects that have failed due to political factors in host countries include Zhongkun Group's investment in Iceland's Grimstadil Tourism Project and Sany Heavy Industry-affiliate Ralls' investment in US wind power, though Sany later filed a lawsuit and later eventually reconciled with the US government. In addition to political risks affecting companies' operations, political risk can also endanger company representatives. On November 21, 2015, three senior executives of China Railway Construction were killed in Mali for political reasons.

According to CCG statistics, from January 1, 2005 to June 30, 2014, in OFDI cases, 25% of Chinese companies' overseas investments that failed were due to political reasons, of which 8% of cases were impacted by the obstruction of host country political factions and 17% suffered losses due to political turmoil in the host country or changes in leadership.

Overseas political risks not only affect the confidence of enterprises in their overseas investments, but also increase labor and financial costs of enterprises' overseas ventures. Therefore, analyzing the sources of political risk for Chinese enterprises' overseas investment and putting forward suggestions to best mitigate these risks is an important task to help enterprises develop sustainable globalization strategies.

3.2.2 *Causal Analysis: Lack of Preparatory Intelligence Gathering and an Imperfect System of Protective Policies*

Firstly, companies need to invest more in gathering intelligence on the political environment in host countries. Insufficient monitoring of the political environment of target countries directly affects the effective development of Chinese enterprises' overseas investment projects. In addition, enterprises are not sufficiently aware of the options available to purchase consulting services, which are a potentially costly but effective means to gain insight into target countries. The lack of professional analysis of the host country's political and policy environment impairs enterprises' ability to assess political risks.

Secondly, companies lack methods and solutions to deal with political risks. Chinese companies going global have limited experience in dealing with political risks, resulting in an insufficient ability to formulate solutions to such crises. The post-event information sharing awareness and capabilities between enterprises appear severely underdeveloped. Companies do not focus on summarizing and learning from crises they encounter, thereby inhibiting subsequent prevention, filing and adjustments.

Thirdly, China's overseas investment security regulations are incomplete and lack cohesion. Neither the "Investment Risk (Political Risk) Clause" formulated by the People's Insurance Company of China in 1983 or the "Insurance Law" promulgated in 1995 provide preventive or protective measures against political risks faced by Chinese investors investing abroad. As a consequence, when cross-border M&As encounter problems, Chinese companies often suffer huge losses due to the lack of relevant legal protection.

3.2.3 *Suggested Solutions*

For enterprises, the first suggestion is to establish and improve overseas security management systems and emergency response mechanisms for overseas security and political emergencies. This includes implementing security risk assessments, planning and formulating overseas security crisis solutions, securing sufficient funds for overseas security issues, and improving overall levels of security.

Secondly, Chinese enterprises should purchase overseas investment insurance and investment security services from reputable providers. Chinese companies should carefully select insurance companies, make full use of the overseas investment insurance system, and develop understanding and use of investment security services. For example, COSCO Shipping Company employs armed security as part of the company's safety management system, requiring subordinate vessels to actively cooperate with armed security and allowing them to systematically conduct safety management on board their ships. In 2011, after the "Leli Wheel" was ambushed by pirates in the Indian Ocean, COSCO Shipping's armed security onboard the vessel were able to counter and successfully repulse the attack.

The third suggestion to mitigate political risk is for Chinese companies to further utilize multilateral investment guarantee institutions. Political risks can be reduced by guarantees provided by multilateral organizations. An example is the World Bank Group's Multilateral Investment Guarantee Agency (MIGA). Compared with the general overseas investment insurance system, MIGA is highly binding on host countries, using multiple prevention measures to mitigate political risks encountered by enterprises in the investment process. At the same time, as an international economic organization and a third-party organization, MIGA's mediation causes minimal damage between the investor and host country, which is conducive to the resolution of political problems. In addition, the range of political risks covered by MIGA is wider than that of general overseas investment insurance and can be extended to other non-commercial risks.

For the Chinese government, there is a need to establish and improve insurance mechanisms regarding political risks faced by corporations in overseas ventures. The government should strive to encourage Chinese insurance companies to expand their foreign investment insurance business and build a comprehensive, multi-level insurance system for enterprises "going global." Moreover, the government should develop and establish policy- and commerce-focused overseas political risk insurance, taking the lead in setting up dedicated foreign investment fund projects. Furthermore, the global sub-insurance and reinsurance business should follow suit to further redistribute the risk of foreign investment.

Secondly, the Chinese government should seek to sign bilateral investment guarantee agreements with host countries. IIAs are important inerantional norms for investment regulation, protection and promotion, including bilateral, regional and multilateral investment agreements, with the bilateral one being the most popular. At present, 56 countries along the "Belt and Road Initiative" route have signed bilateral investment treaties with China. However, most of the agreements were signed in the 1980s and 1990s, and the degree of protection provided to investors is relatively low. Negotiations on upgrading thus should be launched as soon as possible to better adapt the new situation regarding two-way investment by both sides.

Thirdly, China should establish a loss reserve system as soon as possible. To promote overseas investment by domestic enterprises, the Japanese government began to establish a foreign investment loss reserve policy in 1964, especially for enterprises that invest in developing countries or regions with political and economic instability. In 1973, Japan consolidated the overseas investment loss reserve system and the resource investment loss reserve system, establishing a comprehensive foreign investment loss reserve system. Similarly, China should build its own overseas investment loss reserve system to compensate for the losses of "go global" enterprises caused by overseas political crises.

In terms of other organizations, the Bank of China Insurance Supervision and Management Committee should continue to formulate insurance industry information standards and establish insurance risk assessment, early warning and monitoring systems to track, analyze, monitor and guide the operations of the insurance market. China should participate in the formulation of rules of the International Association of Insurance Supervisors (IAIS), as well as strengthen exchange and cooperation with international insurance regulatory agencies. China should also promote the work of the Asian Insurance Supervisor Forum (AFIR) Secretariat in order to enhance China's voice in the formulation of international insurance regulatory rules.

At the same time, it is important to establish bilateral and multilateral regulatory cooperation mechanisms with insurance regulatory agencies in developed countries and regions. Furthermore, China's export credit insurance companies should aim to build a global recovery channel for all types of insurance and cross-sector organizations to form a comprehensive risk management system of diversified risks. Correspondingly, Chinese insurance regulators and providers should make efforts to optimize and upgrade product-service systems, improve information systems and safety management, and improve e-commerce platform services.

3.3 Chinese Investment in the US Under the China-US Trade Issues

3.3.1 Current Situation: Problems Facing Chinese Investment in the US Under the China-US Trade Issues

According to data from the US Department of Commerce, from January to September 2015, China-US trade in goods amounted to US$441.6 billion, marking the start of the era of China and the United States being each other's largest trade partners. The US has always been one of the most popular destinations for Chinese overseas investment. However, on March 22, 2018, the US Trade Representative Office (USTR) published "Article 301: a Survey of China's Trade Practices", which concluded that the Chinese government's actions, policies and practices related to technology transfer, intellectual property rights and innovation were "unreasonable or discriminatory and imposed burdens or restrictions on US commerce". Following this judgment, the US decided to impose tariffs of US$50 billion on Chinese goods and limitations on Chinese investment in the US. As a countermeasure, on April 4 that year, China decided to impose tariffs on US$50 billion of Chinese imports from the US.

Since that point, trade frictions between the two countries have evolved and escalated. On April 5, Trump asked USTR to impose additional tariffs on US$100 billion of Chinese goods. On July 10, the US announced that it would impose further tariffs on China and Canada, imposing a 10% tariff on about US$200 billion worth of Chinese products, then on August 2 increasing this a further 15% to a total of 25%. The trade frictions and imposition of tariffs are heavy blows to the main vehicle of China-US economic relations, namely enterprises from both countries.

The start of China-US trade frictions coincided with increasingly protectionist US investment policy. In August 2018, the "United States Foreign Investment Risk Review Modernization Act" (FIRRMA), part of the "National Defense Authorization Act" (NDAA) of the 2019 fiscal year, was signed and enacted by President Trump. The bill enlarged the jurisdiction of the Committee of Foreign Investment in the United States (CFIUS), enhancing its powers to review investment and making the review process more complex. The CFUIS's expanded jurisdiction means that past transaction information, which companies did not need to declare previously, will also be scrutinized by the CFIUS. This lengthens the review process, increasing wait times and costs for investors. The bill also fails to provide a clear definition for terms such as "national security," "key technologies" or "critical infrastructure." Investments touching on these areas must be reviewed by the CFUIS, thereby giving it the ability to impose subjective restrictions on specific investments. The introduction of this bill will increase difficulties and risks for Chinese enterprises investing in the US.

3.3.2 Causal Analysis: Structural Problems Caused by Rapid Development of the Global Economy, Skewing of China-US Trade Deficit Under Traditional Statistical Methods, and Changes in Domestic and International Politics

To help avoid severe adverse impacts of the China-US trade frictions on the companies of both nations, it is crucial to analyze the underlying causes of the friction.

Firstly, the China-US trade imbalance can be seen as a structural problem caused by the rapid development of the global economy. The trade deficit is shaped by the international division of labor. The industrial structures of the US and China differ significantly; agriculture and manufacturing contribute the most to the Chinese economy, while the most productive area of the US economy is services. In 2016, the US service trade surplus reached US$249.4 billion, whereas China's service trade deficit was US$240.9 billion. The economic structures of China and the US appear to be complementary, as reflected in bilateral trade figures. In the trade of goods, the US runs a deficit, while in the trade of services, China is in deficit.

The US trade deficit with China can also be attributed to the dominant position of the US dollar as the world's currency. In economics, the Triffin Dilemma shows that once a country's currency becomes an international reserve currency, this will cause a trade deficit for that country. If the US did not maintain a trade deficit, the liquidity of the dollar would decrease, having a negative impact on global trade.

Falling household savings and soaring national debt in the US has also widened the trade gap, as have US export controls. In 2001, 16.7% of China's technology imports came from the US. However, by 2016, this had dropped to 8.2%. This trend runs counter to the status of the US as a technological power and important trading partner for China. According to a report by the Carnegie Foundation for International Peace published in April 2017, if US export controls on Chinese goods were reduced to the level of that applied to Brazil, the US-China trade deficit could be reduced by up to 24%. If reduced to the level of that applied to France, the bilateral deficit could be reduced by up to 34%.

A second point to note is that traditional statistical methods have proven to be inaccurate in calculating the US-China trade deficit. There are differences between both sides in key statistics which determine the trade deficit. According to China Customs statistics, in 2017, the US-China trade deficit in goods was US$275.8 billion, not US$375.2 billion as reported by the US. Furthermore, US "Principle of Origin" statistics show that the US has a surplus of up to US$32 billion with Hong Kong. However, the US$100 billion of indirect exports from Hong Kong, Macao and Chinese origins outside of mainland China are not accounted for in the China-US trade volume. If trade is calculated in terms of added value, the US-China deficit would shrink substantially. According to Deutsche Bank's estimates, if the "added value" factor is taken into account, the actual US trade deficit with China in 2017 would have been around US$31 billion, based on the premise that the export structure would not change significantly.

Furthermore, many American and Chinese products in circulation around the globe include parts from both China and the US. For example, Intel supplies chips to ten Apple factories, three in the United States and two in China. The US occupies the middle and high end of many global value chains, engaging in high value-added design and research and design (R&D) activities. China tends to be at the middle to low end, engaged in low-cost production and assembly activities. The two nations are intimately linked in this respect. Foreign-invested enterprises form the key part of China's trade surplus with the US, yet US punitive measures target global industrial chains and value chains.

Indeed, data shows that US-invested enterprises reap the most profits from China-US trade. A 2010 study by the Asian Development Bank showed that American importers and retailers accounted for 90% of the total profits made from Chinese exports of textiles, clothing, shoes and hats. Another typical example is Apple's iPhone. Compared to the US$999 launch price of an iPhone X, it is estimated that manufacturing in China only accounts for 3–6% of the total cost of US$370, translating into a huge profit for Apple. In 2017, the enterprises exporting the most from China in terms of value were mostly foreign-invested enterprises. In light of this, while the "trade surplus" of the global value chain may appear in China, the "profit surplus" is often captured by the US.

Changes in the domestic and international political and economic environment are a fundamental factor in China-US trade tensions. Specifically, changes in US domestic politics were a driving force in fomenting the conflict and shifting the political foundations of bilateral economic relations. Dani Rodrik, Harvard professor and renowned political economist, argues that trade policy has a profound impact on wealth redistribution within countries. Economic globalization has created "winners" and "losers" in the US. The rift between so-called "elite America" and "traditional America" caused by issues related to unequal wealth distribution and social justice contributed to President Trump's election and subsequent trade policies.

Another factor leading to trade frictions was the shift in China-US economic relations, which are increasingly characterized by competition as well as cooperation. In the 1990s, the contribution of the US to global economic growth was 29.1%, while developed western economies, which were represented by the G7, accounted for 76%. From 2008 to 2016, the contribution of the US and developed countries to the world economy declined to 7.4% and 23.9% respectively, while that of China, emerging economies and developing countries rose to 35.6% and 77.7% respectively. This shift reflected the relative rise of the East compared to the West.

China overtook the UK in GDP terms in 2005, Germany in 2007, and replaced Japan as the world's second-largest economy in 2010. In 2012, China's total economic output reached half of that of the US, rising to two-thirds by 2017. Although there is still a considerable gap between China and the US in terms of per capita income, the two nation's economies are similar in size and China is catching up in the development of science and technology.

These factors, in addition to China's growing influence in the international arena, have framed the US-China relationship as one of "competition" in the minds of many of the American elite and general public. Underlying factors behind the trade frictions are linked to a structural tension, namely that of a rising China rivaling US dominance and whether the two nations can co-exist peacefully. The fear that they will not be able to is captured in the "Thucydides trap" theory. Supported by many western scholars, this theory is based on a geopolitical perspective and historical analysis of rising powers. It suggests that China and the US will fall into a new Cold War. Framed in this way, the US' decision to launch a trade frictions can be viewed as a means to "contain" China's rise.

3.3.3 Suggested Solutions

For Chinese enterprises, there are several ways to address the challenges outlined above. Firstly, Chinese companies should strive to adapt to US society and business culture, taking onboard concepts such as corporate social responsibility (CSR) to gain support for their future business activities with and in the US Whilst many Chinese enterprises operating in the US enjoy a good reputation and are deemed strong back home in China, they may be viewed differently in the US market. To win the trust of the American government and people, Chinese companies should follow US business customs and learn to take relevant steps to build trust and relationships. For example, Chinese firms in the US can undertake CSR activities, establish foundations, support local education, help poverty alleviation, and provide quality after-sales services. Building local community relations and favorable public perceptions could help mitigate adverse impacts if the US government turns hostile against Chinese enterprises.

With protectionist policies emerging in the US and other western countries, Chinese companies should actively support multilateralism and seek win-win cooperation with western partners. At the same time, they should consolidate and strengthen ties with the rest of the world and tap the investment potential of emerging economies in Asia, Africa and Latin America. For example, Africa has great development potential. According to the IMF, in 2017, Africa's economy grew 3.7% to US$2.19 trillion. Young people account for over 60% of the continent's 1.25 billion population, providing a strong, growing labor force. At the same time, Africa is rich in resources, its market is growing and the investment environment is gradually improving. In 2012, the African Union (AU) adopted the Program for Infrastructure Development in Africa (PIDA, 2012–2040). The total investment for this program is expected to reach US$360 billion, with an annual funding gap of over US$30 billion for outside investment. Considering Africa's development potential, there is great potential for Chinese enterprises to invest in Africa and African infrastructure in the future, and this program will become an important vehicle for Chinese enterprises to invest in these areas.

The government should provide comprehensive support for Chinese enterprises "going global." The internationalization of Chinese companies is the main force for China's economic integration with the world, directly feeding China's economic globalization. Therefore, the government needs to actively support the overseas development of Chinese enterprises to boost China's global integration and economic outlook. This means actively negotiating with US trade representatives to bring a timely end to the trade frictions.

In addition, the government can continue to safeguard multilateral mechanisms and promote international systems of free trade. Multilateral institutions are crucial for economic development and will continue to play an important role in the future. China must work with partners such as the EU and Japan to support multilateralism, while contributing and putting forward proposals promoting these ideals in multilateral organizations such as the UN, the WTO, the IMF and the G20. For example, to improve its image with respect to intellectual property protection, China can increase participation and promote its achievements through relevant platforms such as the UN World Intellectual Property Organization (WIPO).

To strengthen its multilateral trade links and support the globalization of Chinese firms, China should also consider joining the Comprehensive and Progressive Agreement for Trans-Pacific Partnership (CPTPP), formerly the Trans-Pacific Partnership (TPP). This could improve trade relations with neighbors and also boost China's international position as a leading proponent of free trade. In addition, there is a potential for the CPTPP to eventually be integrated into the Regional Comprehensive Economic Partnership (RCEP) and Free Trade Area of the Asia Pacific (FTAAP), all of which seek to reduce tariffs and remove barriers to trade.

Chinese think tanks, trade associations and other organizations should engage in "track II" diplomacy by strengthening international exchange and opening flexible communication channels with international partners to foster trust and expand engagement. In this way, think tanks and other organizations can help to overcome misunderstandings, bridge differences and provide policy advice. American think tanks such as the Hudson Institute, Heritage Foundation, American Enterprise Institute and Council on Foreign Relations, all have varying levels of influence on the Trump administration's decision-making. Indeed, some government officials hail from these organizations. Through dialogue with these organizations, Chinese think tanks can strengthen exchange between experts and key figures across various fields, playing a role in removing economic and political barriers to deeper engagement. Fulfilling this role requires that Chinese think tanks adopt a more global perspective, pushing them to learn from their international peers. In turn, this would feed into their research and policy work. If Chinese and American think tanks can reach a consensus, this could positively reflect and reinforce the ability of the Chinese and American governments to do the same.

3.4 International Standard Setting

3.4.1 Current Situation: Low-Level of Involvement in International Standard Setting

In October 2015, China released the "Universal Criteria Action Plan for the Belt and Road Initiative," aiming to standardize various aspects of the BRI. Standardization plays an important role in helping Chinese enterprises "go global," providing routes for companies to engage in bilateral and multilateral cooperation across various countries and regions, facilitating investment and trade.

For example, the International Organization for Standardization (ISO) is an important organization in this field. More than 20,000 standards and procedures outlined by the ISO have been adopted by the vast majority of countries and regions in the world. As of March 2016, China had undertaken 50 secretariats of ISO technical committees and participated in 626 activities in ISO technical institutions. However, although China's participation in international standardization activities has made considerable progress in recent years, it still lags behind the US, Germany, the UK, France, Japan and other countries. In 2015, China had the second-largest GDP in the world, while its participation in international standardization ranked sixth (Fig. 3.1).

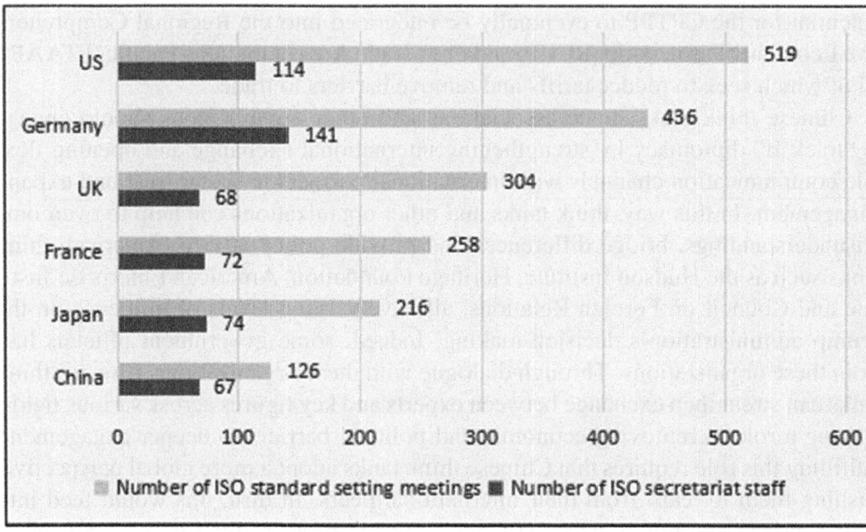

Fig. 3.1 ISO member country contribution rankings. *Source* International Standardization Organization (ISO)

The low level of participation in the formulation of international standards will inhibit the operation and overseas development of Chinese enterprises. Furthermore, if Chinese enterprises are not familiar with international standards and procedures, this will impact their capabilities regarding foreign investment projects and bidding processes. Moreover, there is no requirement to adopt certain standards; it is only through their usage that they become international standards. Therefore, as China has advanced manufacturing technology, if China's standards are not developed and packaged for use overseas, this could weaken the position of Chinese firms with respect to overseas investment.

3.4.2 Causal Analysis: Insufficient Talent, Technology and Funding Lead to Weaknesses in the Content and Translation of Standards

At present in China, there is a lack of funding and qualified personnel engaged in the formulation of standards. Due to the high cost and long-term investment involved in training personnel and lack of developed mechanisms and research in standards formulation, China has struggled to establish a network of talent specialized in this area. This leads to challenges in meeting the needs of China's standardization strategy in terms of quality and quantity. On the one hand, there is insufficient research on internationalizing standardization. On the other hand, the funding provided by the Ministry of Finance is insufficient compared to the actual requirements of strengthening China's standardization practices and development.

Secondly, there remains scope for improvement in the content and structure of some Chinese standards. In some cases, inconsistent technical requirements are included within the standards for one procedure. Sometimes, guidelines, instructions, manuals and reference materials are combined with mandatory standards, further complicating their formulation, preparation and implementation.

In addition, Chinese standards are often mistranslated or use terminology that is not aligned with international standards. This, coupled with the shortage of professionals engaged in the translation of standards, causes significant difficulties, not only in the translation of Chinese standards for the international audience but also for international standards being translated into Chinese. Therefore, strengthening the translation of Chinese standards is one of the most urgent tasks needed to internationalize Chinese standards.

3.4.3 Suggested Solutions

To address the issue of Chinese standards formulation, it is necessary for industry, government and standardization organizations to work together.

Chinese enterprises should continue to formulate and revise existing standards and expand inter-industry technology exchange. Based on market demand, Chinese companies should formulate and revise product standards and seek to establish an effective system of standards. At the same time, standardization should be promoted in industry, with various forms of standardization used to support product development and innovation. In addition, enterprises should establish industry standard alliances that facilitate technology exchange and information-sharing among enterprises and lead in formulating industry standards.

Efforts should be made to boost professionalization in the translation of Chinese and English standards, improve verification work in comparing Chinese and foreign standards, and align the main components of Chinese standards with relevant standards used in Europe, America and Japan. By using professional standard translation agencies, Chinese companies can ensure the accuracy and standardization of translations. For standard comparison and verification, enterprises should actively engage with foreign chambers of commerce, owners and relevant organizations to discuss and judge the national comparability of standards. By expanding international exchange with leading countries in standards such as European countries, the US and Japan, Chinese companies will be able to gain a better grasp of language and other norms associated with international standard setting.

Firms should also take steps to demonstrate applications for standard implementation and strengthen research on the promotion and application of standards. Once standards reach the stage of application, companies responsible for the formulation of the standard should create clear guidance on how the standard should be applied, in accordance with international standard guidelines. This can be achieved through better translation and more focus on providing demonstrations and examples of the standard in action. For example, the efficacy of the standard can be demonstrated through product result samples and promoted by sharing finished products with potential international partners to increase awareness and understanding of Chinese standards and product quality.

For its part, the government should support standards development through increased spending on building China's standard formulation systems, training talent, and procurement. These efforts should be focused on standardization training, in particular, training and acquiring high-end talent familiar with international standards. Relevant government bodies should establish a sustainable talent training mechanism, training a group of interdisciplinary experts with strong language capabilities that understand international norms and procedures to strengthen China's standardization community. At the same time, multichannel funding support should be introduced, not only to increase overall funding, but also to ensure that special funds are used exclusively for their intended purpose and in a transparent, fair and efficient manner.

The government should also support wider international engagement, working to set up organizations and research institutions focused on formulating standards and strengthening standardization. There should be top-down promotion to deepen Chinese engagement with international standard organizations such as the ISO, the International Electrotechnical Commission (IEC), the International Telecommunication Union (ITU). Increased participation in such organizations will boost China's ability to contribute to international standard formulation. Engagement at this level will also help the international recognition of Chinese national standards.

Finally, the government should pursue international cooperation between Chinese standard formulation bodies and international partners to promote the internationalization of Chinese standards. There are various opportunities for cooperation through BRI projects. This type of cooperation could strengthen cohesion and linkages in standards among countries and regions engaged in the initiative. Related government departments should take the lead in encouraging the adoption of Chinese standards overseas by promoting the use of Chinese design and construction, equipment and services in overseas projects, highways, railways and other forms of foreign investment, especially in areas where China has unique advantages.

Institutions related to standards formulation and promotion need to take steps to optimize their organizational structure, research and standards adoption. The Standardization Administration of China needs to build and manage an efficient and authoritative system to coordinate standardization. This can be achieved by streamlining current applicable standards and gradually integrating them into a national standard system; establishing industry standards; and relaxing restrictive or unnecessary standards for enterprises. Through these efforts, a new national standardization system will be established by 2020, with government-led standardization regulations working in coordination with industry-formulated standards and practices.

The Standardization Administration should coordinate activities relating to the development of Chinese standards, practice and standardization procedures. This includes promoting international exchange with standardization experts, academic debate and research, and working with relevant government departments to produce laws and regulations on standards. These efforts should be focused in areas where China has unique advantages and aims to develop further, such as in the standardization of scientific research, demonstrated in scientific and technological projects, and the appraisal of standardized scientific and technological achievements.

3.5 Internationalization of Chinese Brands

3.5.1 Current Situation: Chinese Brand Internationalization Strategies Face Obstacles

The World Brand Lab's 2017 "500 Most Influential Brands" ranking names the US as the most influential branding nation, with 233 brands on the list. France comes in second with 40 brands, the UK third with 39, with China following behind with 37 brands listed. This fourth-place ranking does not match up to China's status as the world's second-largest economy. Leading global market research firm Millward Brown, in its annual "Brandz 100 Most Valuable Global Brands" 2018 report, only listed 15 Chinese brands in its rankings. Of these, Tencent was the highest-ranked Chinese brand, valued at US$178 billion, just 59% of the value of the top-ranked company, Google (Figs. 3.2 and 3.3).

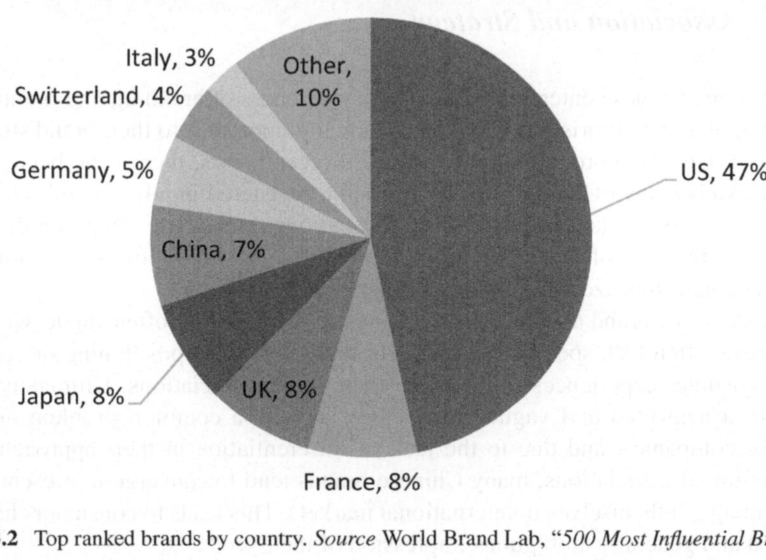

Fig. 3.2 Top ranked brands by country. *Source* World Brand Lab, "*500 Most Influential Brands*"

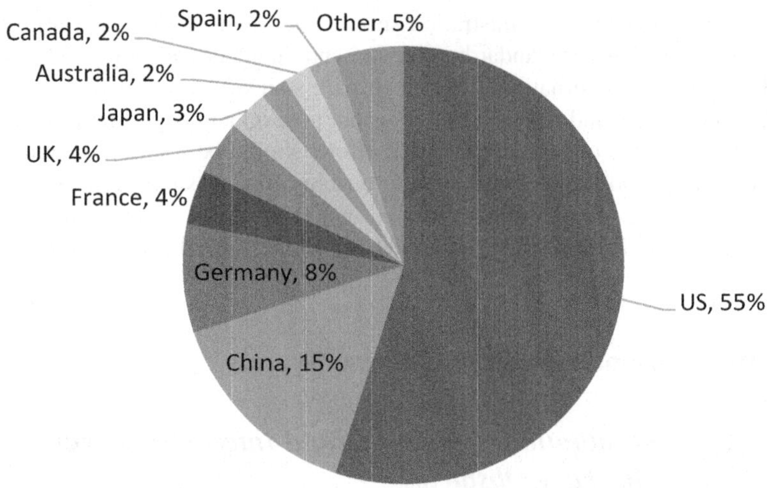

Fig. 3.3 Most valuable global brands by country. *Source* Millwall Brown "*Brandz 2018 100 Most Valuable Brands*" ranking

Globalizing Chinese firms with less influential brands will struggle to gain a significant share of the global market. Weak brand strategies impair the international competitiveness of Chinese firms. This highlights the importance of formulating a strong brand internationalization strategy for Chinese enterprises "going global."

3.5.2 Causal Analysis: Lack of Brand Awareness, Association and Strategy

Firstly, some Chinese enterprises have weak awareness of branding and brand protection. Chinese enterprises do not attach enough importance to their brand strategy and pay relatively more attention to sales. In recent years, there have been many cases of well-known Chinese trademarks being registered in advance by others in the international market. In addition to this, national brands are often in a difficult position in the face of large inflows of foreign brands, which limits the ability of Chinese brands to seize international market share.

Secondly, the brand associations of Chinese enterprises are often vague. Chinese enterprises often lack specific cultural definitions for brand positioning or support from consumer experiences to reinforce their brand associations. Ultimately, this leads to a neglected and vague brand ethos. This is a common problem among Chinese companies, and due to the lack of differentiation in their approaches in shaping brand associations, many Chinese brands tend to converge in presenting a vague image of themselves in international markets. This leads to consumers having a mixed and generally ambiguous impression of their products.

Finally, Chinese enterprises lack effective branding and marketing strategy. Brand visualization should be completed before marketing, as this can aid in the building of sales networks through brand integration, forming an effective strategy to rapidly expand brand awareness. However, after an overseas merger or acquisition by a Chinese enterprise, it may be difficult for enterprises to decide whether to use a single unified brand marketing strategy or keep newly acquired brands separate from the Chinese parent brand. For Chinese enterprises "going global," the dual-brand strategy is a double-edged sword. Such strategies require that companies overcome the brand awareness gap and also dilute resources available for R&D and sales across two brands, which may affect the overall benefits accrued from this type of merger and acquisition.

3.5.3 Suggested Solutions

Chinese enterprises should pay more attention to brand development, focusing on brand associations to bolster brand awareness and future strategy. Enterprises should know how to shape brand association while representing and differentiating their brand values from others. In shaping brand connotations, the most valuable characteristics can be identified through detailed internal and external analysis, especially through interviews with customers and leading enterprises in the industry. At the same time, Chinese companies should use customer value orientations to guide their brand association strategy. Through these, brands can distinguish different types of consumer needs and target customers with more effective marketing. On this basis, by dividing single and double brands into hierarchical markets, different customer groups can be outlined. This will help to maintain brand integrity and ensure core brand competencies.

Secondly, brand internationalization strategies should involve constant innovation of products and marketing methods, maintain branding consistency across campaigns, and establish models of engagement conducive to brand integrity. Therefore, while focusing on product innovation, there needs to be careful conception and design of products and marketing campaigns, taking into account differences related to culture, language, government regulations, advertising, and media.

Finally, for all brands, it is crucial to build up sales networks and strength brand marketing strategy. Brand mergers and acquisitions and brand alliances are some of the methods enterprises can use to expand and enhance their strength and efficiency. For example, Japan's nine major conglomerates have more than 150 branches and agents all over the world, promoting Japanese products around the globe. Chinese enterprises can also expand into foreign markets more quickly through Sino-foreign joint ventures, directly utilizing the sales networks of local brands. Leading Chinese brand Haier's acquisition of GE's household appliances assets in 2016 will enable it to quickly penetrate North American and Latin American markets by leveraging GE's established brand image, existing sales channels, retailer relations, first-class distribution capabilities, and global footprint.

The government can assist brand internationalization by strengthening legislation relating to intellectual property rights and brand development to support fair competition. Brand promotion and development centers could be established in certain regions for specific industries. Exchange between Chinese enterprises can be expanded by establishing specialized national brand management institutions and forming brand industry alliances. Related government departments should also build industry exhibition platforms, making use of international forums and exhibitions for overseas promotion of Chinese brands. At international forums, exhibitions and trade fairs, Chinese brands should not only display new products and advanced technologies, but also seek to convey brand concepts to international media and consumers.

Industry bodies and chambers of commerce also have a role to play. To support branding efforts, these organizations should work together to establish R&D centers or collaboration centers applying international-level advanced technologies and standards. These bodies should also carry out exchanges with their international counterparts. They should encourage cooperation between Chinese brands and overseas peers to develop branding strategies, learn overseas brand management, and share experiences so as to promote greater implementation of brand strategy across the whole industry.

3.6 Talent Internationalization

3.6.1 Current Situation: Chinese Enterprises Lack International Talent

At present, there is a serious problem of low internationalization of talent in Chinese enterprises. According to the McKinsey report "Addressing China's Looming Talent Shortage", China is seriously short of interdisciplinary managerial personnel to meet the skills requirements of multinational operations. It is estimated that by 2020, China will need 75,000 managers with international experience, while at present, China has only 5,000 such personnel.[1] Moreover, a survey titled "China Enterprise Strategy: Current Situation, Problems and Suggestions—Special Report on the Growth and Development of Chinese Enterprise Managers in 2010", published by the Chinese Entrepreneur Survey System, shows that 64.5% of enterprise managers believe that the lack of qualified international talent is the biggest difficulty for enterprise internationalization. Meanwhile, according to the "Development Report on China's Top 500 Enterprises 2018" and the "World Investment Report 2018" issued by UNCTAD, the average proportion of "internationalized" employees in 10 large-scale global companies was 94.72%, while the average proportion of internationalized employees in 10 large-scale Chinese companies was only 45.40% (Table 3.1). It can be seen that

[1] McKinsey Official Website, http://www.mckinseychina.com/.

Table 3.1 2018 comparison of international and Chinese multinational company employee internationalization

Ranking		Company name	No. of employees	No. of intl. employees	Percent of employee internation-alization (%)
Top 10 Global Multinational Companies 2018					
1	99.4	Rio Tinto PLC	46807	46498	99.34
2	98.6	John Swire & Sons Limited	80820	80707	99.86
3	96.2	Broadcom Limited	14000	13100	93.57
4	96.1	Anglo American PLC	69000	67000	97.10
5	94.8	British American Tobacco	91402	78843	86.26
6	94.8	Altice NV	47173	45454	96.36
7	91.8	Nestle	323000	312867	96.86
8	91.3	Schneider Electric	153124	134749	88.00
9	91.1	Nokia	101731	95372	93.75
10	89.8	Medtronic, Inc.	91000	87432	96.08
Average rate of employee internationalization					94.72
Top 10 Chinese Multinational Companies 2018					
1	70.43	China National Chemical Corporation Ltd.	138185	85987	62.23
2	63.89	WH Group	110000	53000	48.18
3	59.67	Sinochem Group	62006	8909	14.37
4	54.90	Lenovo	444000	146643	33.03
5	54.16	Geely Auto	80914	32932	40.70
6	52.23	Joyson Electronics	28349	22056	77.80
7	51.60	Haier	74570	42858	57.47
8	49.73	Zhongding Group	15002	7075	47.16
9	45.96	Fosun	53000	20457	38.60
10	44.37	Jinko Solar	12696	4373	34.44
Average rate of employee internationalization					45.40

Source China Enterprise Confederation, China Entrepreneurs Association: "*Development Report on China's Top 500 Enterprises 2018*"; UNCTAD "*World Investment Report 2018*"

the level of internationalization of employees in Chinese multinationals is far below the global average.

The discussion above highlights how the international talent gap is one of the main restrictions for Chinese enterprises investing abroad and improving management of overseas assets and operations.

3.6.2 Causal Analysis: Weak Human Resources Management and Cultivation

On the whole, Chinese human resources (HR) management appears to be failing to engage with international talent. The HR management challenges for "go global" enterprises are reflected in the lack of understanding of overseas labor markets and local laws and regulations, as well as clear differences between Chinese and international HR systems and management. Differences in organization hierarchy, standard mechanisms of employee evaluation, salary management and work-life balance create gaps between Chinese employers and international employees.

Secondly, mechanisms to attract and retain international employees are yet to be established in many Chinese companies. Improvements in this area face significant obstacles. Tax rates imposed on international employees are high and there is a lack of incentives and mechanisms to recruit international employees. Moreover, attractive remuneration packages are not viable under the current tax system, especially generous salary and incentive packages for international employees that are subject to high taxes, raising the cost of retaining international talent. In addition, there are few social security and medical insurance systems catering for international employees. Most highly-skilled workers in China purchase private medical insurance, with their employer paying in part. With rising medical costs, there has been a noted increase of international employees having disputes with insurance companies and their employers over medical payments, dissuading international talent from working in Chinese companies.

3.6.3 Suggested Solutions

One key way enterprises can attract and retain international talent is to improve localization and create a more inclusive corporate culture. After an overseas merger or acquisition, it is important for the Chinese company to retain the local corporate culture, being sensitive of cultural differences and cultural integration. For example, when the Chinese construction company Zoomlion purchased and merged with CIFA, one of the world's largest concrete machinery manufacturers, they committed not to lay off any staff and made no major changes to local management teams. By appreciating cultural diversity and being aware of localization challenges, the company has been able to achieve great success in its cultural integration efforts.[2] In addition, enterprises should help to strengthen the localization of their employees. For example, companies can establish "management colleges" or "training centers" to provide personnel training and also to support investment destination partners, suppliers, distributors, customers and local officials and provide training to guide and cultivate internal and external corporate cultural identity.

Secondly, companies should seek to develop and utilize their international employees, including overseas Chinese and Chinese employees who have studied abroad, while also looking to internationalize and have independent figures on their board of directors. Research shows that having an internationalized senior leadership team is a necessary condition for effective implementation of internationalization strategy, helping to eliminate constraints of narrow regional perspectives and establish a global outlook.[3] Boards of directors with more internationalized knowledge and skills invest more time in internationalization strategy, in turn boosting the internationalization of operations and management.[4] At present, it is uncommon for Chinese local enterprises to employ international employees as senior managers. As Chinese enterprises enter the global market and provide global services, they must look to internationalize management and attach more value to international work experience.

While internationalizing management, HR departments should also seek to internationalize themselves. This is a necessary transformation in the course of an enterprise's globalization. To achieve this, the payment structure in Chinese enterprises needs to keep pace with international standards. When recruiting international employees, Chinese companies need to match global, not Chinese standards, and offer internationally competitive salaries.

For its part, the government should pay attention to immigration management, especially the reform of China's green card system. To attract more overseas talent to China, the application scope for green cards should be relaxed appropriately. There should be more focus on providing convenient ways to set up green card processing agencies across the country for international personnel in China. For example, green card application windows could be set up in overseas embassies and consulates. These factors are key to establishing a more systematic and developed policy system for the entry, exit and employment of non-Chinese nationals.

The government should also seek to fully utilize former Chinese diplomats and businesspeople to better improve approaches to internationalization. Often, diplomats and members of chambers of commerce have a strong understanding of the host country and its legal environment, economy, culture, industrial policies and preferential policies. China has tens of thousands of overseas personnel from embassies and consulates. Chinese companies should be given the full opportunity and have platforms where they can utilize these resources, allowing them to play an advisory and consultative role in the process of enterprises "going global."

---

[2]Chen (2012).

[3]Sambharya (1996).

[4]Zhou et al. (2013).

There should also be government support for the overseas development of Chinese recruiters and use of international recruitment services. On the one hand, the government should assist Chinese recruitment agencies to "go global" and enter the international market. On the other hand, the government can cooperate with international recruitment agencies by purchasing their services. Specifically, considering the large number of Chinese enterprises expanding overseas that struggle to recruit and retain high-end talent and provide high-level training, the government could subsidize part of the recruitment costs for these activities. It could encourage Chinese recruitment agencies to set up overseas offices and attract multinational recruitment agencies to China with preferential measures such as tax and housing subsidies.

Chinese recruitment intermediaries and headhunters should also seek to become "localized" in overseas markets to best support Chinese companies as they "go global." Recruitment agencies should cultivate loyal market segments and form unique business models and core competencies to win customer trust. Such organizations could look to establish HR alliances, with recruitment agencies as the main body, strengthening the standardization of talent recruitment search mechanisms and operations.

3.7 Enterprise Compliance

3.7.1 Current Situation: Compliance Is a Critical Component of Chinese Enterprises' Internationalization

Before and after the global financial crisis in 2008, Chinese enterprises have emphasized social and environmental responsibility, making major progress in developing corporate culture. A number of Chinese enterprises have made achievements in building robust compliance management systems. For example, to ensure compliance and mitigate associated risk, China National Petroleum Corporation (CNPC) formulated "CPNC Regulations for Compliance Management" making key leaders of the conglomerate and its affiliated enterprises the first to be held responsible for compliance management.

However, not all enterprises have paid enough attention to strengthening global compliance over the past decade. With stricter supervision of international compliance, the challenges of compliance management for Chinese enterprises "going global" are becoming more pressing. According to a Deloitte survey of about 40 Chinese company executives, only about 50% of the Chinese multinationals surveyed had compliance management responsibilities assumed by independent departments with an independent Chief Compliance Officer that participates in high-level discussions on corporate strategy, values and culture. In many companies, the legal affairs department is responsible for compliance management. More than one-third of enterprises did not use any dedicated information systems or tools in their regulatory management systems. In contrast, many large multinational companies are exploring the use of big data and information technology to collect compliance management data, analyze the effectiveness of compliance management and conduct compliance surveys.

3.7.2 Causal Analysis: Chinese Enterprises Are not Familiar with Overseas Laws and Take Risks Without Having the Necessary Compliance Mechanisms in Place

Chinese companies' lack of familiarity with or neglect of overseas laws and regulations has caused them to encounter legal disputes or huge fines, resulting in serious company losses. For example, European countries attach great importance to the protection of personal data. In 2018, the EU promulgated the "General Data Protection Regulation," which required more stringent protection of personal information. This resulted in Chinese enterprises having to further strengthen their personal data protection and is exactly the type of regulation enterprises need to be fully aware of. At the same time, for relatively smaller-scale enterprises that wish to "go global," it can be difficult to fully grasp local laws and regulations. Such firms may need the help and guidance of relevant service agencies.

Certain enterprises are prone to take risks and rush decision-making in search of profit. According to media reports, some Chinese enterprises overseas win orders or projects through commercial corruption and bribery. This kind of illegal and immoral activity hurts not only their own international image, but also that of other Chinese enterprises. On top of this, Chinese enterprises investing in countries with high levels of corruption are prone to bribe solicitation. Some enterprises take the initiative to carry out commercial bribery to secure business opportunities. This brings high compliance risks for continued overseas operations, and again damages the overall image of Chinese enterprises investing and operating abroad.

Furthermore, the compliance systems of many Chinese enterprises are inadequate and do not effectively prevent illegal activities overseas. In recent years, a series of compliance incidents relating to Chinese enterprises' overseas business activities have occurred. This reflects how Chinese enterprises lack comprehensive compliance mechanisms for overseas business activities and the difficulties they face in adapting to overseas regulatory systems. Effective compliance systems not only enable companies to mitigate risk, but can also become effective tools for defense and trust building for enterprises when they face investigation by law enforcement agencies.

3.7.3 Suggested Solutions

To set up effective compliance mechanisms, Chinese companies need to cultivate a culture of compliance management. The mantra “compliance as the cornerstone of company strategy” should be embedded into company culture. It should permeate all levels of the company and be recognized by all, with each employee realizing that compliance management is an indispensable part of the company’s development. This type of corporate culture can only be established if leadership and management foster the ideas and habits of compliance management, and integrate the concept of compliance management into the corporate culture. To promote honest business practices and behavior, employees should receive dedicated training to keep everyone up to date with compliance regulations and responsibilities.

Building on compliance culture, robust systems and mechanisms must be put in place. This begins with creating a compliance department. Enterprises should establish a full-time specialized compliance department from the outset, giving this department a clear mission, internal control framework, as well as role and function at the strategic level. To ensure the independence of the compliance department, it should report directly to senior managers or the board of directors and maintain its ability and right to work independently without interference. This department’s focus is conducting investigations and researching company activities and projects to identify compliance risks. Key business areas of company management, especially geopolitical conflict areas and areas with high incidences of corruption, should be the focal points of the compliance department’s investigation and research. For compliance work on a departmental level, their focus should be finance, sales, procurement and other business departments. It is through investigation, identification and evaluation carried out by the compliance department that compliance problems and associated risks can be most effectively dealt with.

Once compliance risks are identified, issues highlighted by compliance departments must be acted upon. After establishing a compliance department and systems, enterprises need to internally promote, advocate and effectively implement compliance systems. The implementation of compliance responsibilities should be guaranteed by clear communication and coordination among compliance departments and internal and external stakeholders.

Effective implementation of a compliance management system also hinges on four operational mechanisms, namely: comprehensive training, strict assessment, reporting, and effective investigation and punishment. Effective functioning of these four mechanisms depends to a large extent on whether enterprise leadership act as an example in promoting compliance. Therefore, ensuring the smooth operation of compliance mechanisms requires the enterprise leadership actively promote compliance corporate culture and lead by example. However, due to changing legal and regulatory environments as well as the location of companies’ operations, no compliance system is perfect and it must be constantly updated and adjusted.

The government’s role in this area should be to strengthen relevant legislation on the compliance management of Chinese enterprises. In recent years, the Chinese government has continued to legislate and enforce laws in the field of compliance, aiding enterprises' compliance management. In November 2014, the APEC Ministerial Conference adopted the "Beijing Declaration on Anti-Corruption," which was the first international anti-corruption declaration drafted by the Chinese government. It reflects the consensus reached by APEC economies focusing on anti-corruption cooperation and the future direction of anti-corruption and compliance efforts in the region. In addition to regional efforts, on August 23, 2016, the General Office of the State Council issued "Opinions on Establishing an Investment Responsibility Investigation System for State-owned Enterprises' Illegal Operations", which imposes high standards for Chinese SOEs and strict implementation. It will have a significant positive impact on the compliance of SOEs. On top of this, on May 23, 2017, the 35th meeting of the Leading Group of the Central Committee on Comprehensive and Deepening Reform adopted "Opinions on Regulating the Overseas Business Behavior of Enterprises," which emphasized the need to strengthen compliance systems for Chinese enterprises' overseas business operations. Furthermore, on December 6, 2017, the National Development and Reform Commission, the Ministry of Commerce, the People's Bank of China, the Ministry of Foreign Affairs and the All-China Federation of Industry and Commerce jointly issued the "Code of Conduct for Private Enterprises' Overseas Investment and Operations," which guides private enterprises to operate in total compliance with the law. This declaration states: "Private enterprises and their overseas branches should conscientiously carry out relevant compliance procedures at home and abroad, engage in fair competition and operate in good faith." On December 29, 2017, the national standard GB/T 35770-2017 "Guidelines for Compliance Management Systems," which was formulated by the China National Institute of Standardization, was formally approved and issued by the State Administration of Quality Supervision, Inspection and Quarantine and the Standardization Administration of China, and implemented on July 1, 2018.

In the face of legal and operational irregularities, law enforcement investigations and huge fines faced by Chinese enterprises overseas, the government should take the lead in setting up relevant compliance review committees to supervise the compliance operation of enterprises via the mode of internal supervision. By doing so, the government will aid Chinese companies navigating the minefield of overseas investment, helping to supervise and review crucial aspects of Chinese enterprises "going global." Finally, the government could also assist in training compliance personnel to help enterprises better deal with overseas violations and minimize risks and losses.

The government should also lead central state-owned enterprises to implement compliance systems and launch pilot projects to help enterprises establish their own compliance systems. In addition to the legislation of the National People's Congress, which affects all businesses, guidelines should also be applied within enterprises to regulate internal business practices. For example, in March 2016, China's State-owned Assets Supervision and Administration Commission selected five central state-owned enterprises (PetroChina, China Mobile, China Merchants Group, China Railway and Dongfang Electric) as pilot projects for compliance system development.

Other organizations, such as think tanks, can advise on the development of compliance mechanisms and help enterprises in their global development. As the primary function of most think tanks is to perform research, they can provide well-grounded, objective suggestions for enterprises to help them analyze the relevant legal requirements, investment environment, review priorities and investment trends. Independent and non-governmental think tanks are especially well-placed to provide more neutral and objective consultation services for enterprises. Think tanks also hold diverse perspectives, which is conducive to incorporating different interests and values into their policy analysis and advice. In reviewing the internal management of corporate compliance, think tanks can provide valuable insights from multiple perspectives, such as the investment enterprise, Chinese government, target country, investor government, and public opinion.

References

BITs and the Protection of Overseas Investment Interests: Based on an Analysis of BITs between China and B & R Countries, Han Bing, International Economic Cooperation, No. 8, 2017.

Chen Jie, "The More Localized, The More Internationalized", *The Board of Directors,* 2012, 12, pp. 78–80.

Huiyao Wang, Lu Miao and others, eds, Report on Chinese Enterprises Globalization 2015, Social Sciences Academic Press (China), 2015, p. 205. The statistical sample here is 120 cases of outward investment failure from January 2005 to 30 June 2014.

Sambharya R. B. *Foreign experience of top management teams and international diversification strategies of US multinational corporations[J]*. Strategic Management Journal, 1996.

Zhou Jian, Yin Cuifeng, Chen Surong, "The Impact of Board Characteristics on Internationalization Strategies", *Management Review,* 2013, 11.

Appendix

Statistics on Outbound Investment by Chinese Enterprises 2016–2017

H. Wang and L. Miao, *The Globalization of Chinese Enterprises: Trends and Characteristics*, The Chinese Enterprise Globalization Series,
https://doi.org/10.1007/978-981-15-4646-4

Year	Investor	Counterparty	Transaction amount (million dollars)	Investment method	Industry of investor (first level)	Industry of target	Country/Region of target	Continent
2016	沈阳联立铜业有限公司	哈萨克斯坦中亚黄金集团	480.00	Newly-established	Manufacturing	Mining	Kazakhstan	Asia
2016	CMST Development Co., Ltd.	Mercuria Energy Group Limited	60.00	Merger and acquisition	Transportation, storage and post	Transportation, storage and post	UK	Europe
2016	China Three Gorges Corporation	Brazilian ministry of mines and energy	3700.00	Merger and acquisition	Production and supply of power, gas and water	Production and supply of power, gas and water	Brazil	South America
2016	Ctrip.com International, Ltd.	MakeMyTrip	180.00	Merger and acquisition	Information transmission, computer service and software	Information transmission, computer service and software	India	Asia
2016	Shandong Oriental Ocean Group Co., Ltd.	Avioq		Merger and acquisition	Comprehensive	Manufacturing	USA	North America
2016	China National Chemical Corporation	Onex Corporation	1010.00	Merger and acquisition	Manufacturing	Manufacturing	Germany	Europe
2016	Hailiang International Holdings Ltd.	JMF Company	30.00	Merger and acquisition	Manufacturing	Manufacturing	USA	North America
2016	Beijing Kunlun Tech CO., Ltd.	New Grindr, LLC	93.00	Merger and acquisition	Information transmission, computer service and software	Information transmission, computer service and software	USA	North America
2016	Shandong Hengyuan Petrochemical Company Limited	Malaysian-Based Shell Refining Company	66.30	Merger and acquisition	Manufacturing	Manufacturing	Malaysia	Asia
2016	China Aerospace Science and Technology Corporation	CNIC Corporation Limited	19.98	Merger and acquisition	Manufacturing	Financial	USA	North America

(continued)

(continued)

Year	Investor	Counterparty	Transaction amount (million dollars)	Investment method	Industry of investor (first level)	Industry of target	Country/Region of target	Continent
2016	China Aerospace Science and Industry Corporation Limited	IEE International Electronics & Engineering	206.73	Merger and acquisition	Manufacturing	Manufacturing	USA	North America
2016	Haier Group	General Electric	5580.00	Merger and acquisition	Manufacturing	Manufacturing	USA	North America
2016	China National Chemical Corporation	Mercuria		Merger and acquisition	Manufacturing	Manufacturing	Switzerland	Europe
2016	Pearl River Piano	Schimmel Pianoforte Beteiligungsgesellschaft mbH & Co KG	27.40	Merger and acquisition	Manufacturing	Manufacturing	Germany	Europe
2016	China Poly Group Corporation Limited	British Land	126.93	Merger and acquisition	Real estate	Real estate	UK	Europe
2016	Sinosteel Corporation	Bolivia	450.00	Newly-established	Manufacturing	Mining	Bolivia	South America
2016	Wanda Group	Haryana, India	10000.00	Newly-established	Comprehensive	Real estate	India	Asia
2016	Silk Road Fund Co., Ltd.	ACWA Power		Newly-established	Financial	Production and supply of power, gas and water	United Arab Emirates	Asia
2016	Visual China Group	Corbis Images		Merger and acquisition	Culture, sport and entertainment	Culture, sport and entertainment	USA	North America
2016	Zhejiang Dingli Machinery Co., Ltd.	Magni	16.08	Merger and acquisition	Manufacturing	Manufacturing	Italy	Europe
2016	Beijing Kunlun Tech Co., Ltd.	Curacloud Group Limited	2.50	Newly-established	Information transmission, computer service and software	Information transmission computer service and software	Cayman Islands	North America

(continued)

(continued)

Year	Investor	Counterparty	Transaction amount (million dollars)	Investment method	Industry of investor (first level)	Industry of target	Country/Region of target	Continent
2016	Liaoning Wangyuhe Investment Co., Ltd.	Sakhalin Government in Russia		Newly-established	Financial	Manufacturing	Russia	Europe
2016	China National Nuclear Power Co., Ltd.		23.37	Newly-established	Production and supply of power, gas and water	Production and supply of power, gas and water	UK	Europe
2016	China Communications Construction Company Ltd.		13.45	Newly-established	Construction	Construction	Maldives	Europe
2016	China Investment Corporation	Qube Holdings Ltd.		Merger and acquisition	Financial	Transportation, storage and post	Australia	Oceania
2016	CHINT ELECTRIC Co., Ltd.	GRABAT ENERGY, S.L.	20.13	Merger and acquisition	Manufacturing	Manufacturing	Spain	Europe
2016	SAIC Motor Corporation Limited	General Motors Corporation		Merger and acquisition	Manufacturing	Manufacturing	India	Asia
2016	Joincare Pharmaceutical Group Industry Co., Ltd.	Apricot Forest	30.00	Merger and acquisition	Manufacturing	Manufacturing	USA	North America
2016	Tianjin Keyvia Electric Co., Ltd.	Balfour Beatty Rail Signal GmbH	20.85	Merger and acquisition	Manufacturing	Manufacturing	Germany	Europe
2016	Tianjin Keyvia Electric Co., Ltd.	BICC Holdings GmbH	0.11	Merger and acquisition	Manufacturing	Manufacturing	Germany	Europe
2016	Tsinghua Unigroup Ltd.	ChipMOS Technologies Inc.	358.33	Merger and acquisition	Manufacturing	Information transmission, computer service and software	Taiwan	Asia
2016	Ningbo Joyson Electronic Corp	KSS Holdings, Inc.	920.00	Merger and acquisition	Manufacturing	Manufacturing	USA	North America
2016	Ningbo Joyson Electronic Corp	TechniSat Digital GmbH, Daun	201.35	Merger and acquisition	Manufacturing	Manufacturing	Germany	Europe
2016	ELLASSAY Co., Ltd.	香港唐利国际控股有限公司	35.48	Merger and acquisition	Manufacturing	Manufacturing	Hong Kong	Asia

(continued)

(continued)

Year	Investor	Counterparty	Transaction amount (million dollars)	Investment method	Industry of investor (first level)	Industry of target	Country/Region of target	Continent
2016	Beijing Jetsen Technology Co., Ltd.	NV Auro Holding	28.00	Merger and acquisition	Information transmission, computer service and software	Information transmission, computer service and software	Belgium	Europe
2016	Mig Technology Co., Ltd.	Tapjoy, Inc.	5.00	Merger and acquisition	Manufacturing	Information transmission,computer service and software	USA	North America
2016	Macrolink Real Estate Co., Ltd.	黑石度假村株式会社		Merger and acquisition	Real estate	Wholesale and retail	Korea	Asia
2016	CITIC Capital, Hua Capital Management Co., Ltd. and Goldstone Investment Limited	OmniVision Technologies, Inc.	1900.00	Merger and acquisition	Financial	Scientific research, technology service and geological survey	USA	North America
2016	Wanda Group	Legendary Pictures	3500.00	Merger and acquisition	Comprehensive	Culture, sport and entertainment	USA	North America
2016	Alibaba Group	Magic Leap	700	Merger and acquisition	Information transmission, computer service and software	Information transmission, computer service and software	USA	North America
2016	China National Chemical Corporation	Syngenta	43000.00	Merger and acquisition	Manufacturing	Manufacturing	Switzerland	Europe
2016	Jiangxi Ganfeng Lithium Co., Ltd.	Reed Industrial Minerals Pty Ltd.	27.15	Merger and acquisition	Manufacturing	Mining	Australia	Oceania

(continued)

(continued)

Year	Investor	Counterparty	Transaction amount (million dollars)	Investment method	Industry of investor (first level)	Industry of target	Country/Region of target	Continent
2016	China Security Co., Ltd.	Guardforce Security Service Company Limited Guardforce Aviation Security Services Limited, Guardforce Aviation Services Limited		Merger and acquisition	Scientific research, technology service and geological survey	Scientific research, technology service and geological survey	Thailand	Asia
2016	HNA Group (International) Company Limited	Azul Brazilian Airlines	450.00	Merger and acquisition	Comprehensive	Transportation, storage and post	Brazil	South America
2016	Suzhou Dongshan Precision Manufacturing Co., Ltd.	Multi-Fineline Electronix Inc.	592.80	Merger and acquisition	Manufacturing	Manufacturing	USA	North America
2016	Shanghai Jin Jiang International Hotels (group) Company Limited	Accor Hotels		Merger and acquisition	Lodging and catering	Lodging and catering	France	Europe
2016	Chengdu Techcent Environment Co., Ltd.	Bilfinger Water Technologies GmbH	229.31	Merger and acquisition	Irrigation, environment and infrastructure management	Irrigation, environment and infrastructure management	Germany	Europe
2016	Chongqing Casin Enterprise Group Co., Ltd.	Chicago Stock Exchange		Merger and acquisition	Financial	Financial	USA	North America
2016	Beijing Enterprises Group Company Limited	EQT Partners Company	1566.05	Merger and acquisition	Financial	Production and supply of power, gas and water	Germany	Europe
2016	Vitajoy Bio-tech Co., Ltd.	WTS(World Trade System PLC)		Merger and acquisition	Wholesale and retail	Financial	UK	Europe
2016	Alibaba Group	Groupon	100.00	Merger and acquisition	Information transmission, computer service and software	Information transmission computer service and software	USA	North America

(continued)

(continued)

Year	Investor	Counterparty	Transaction amount (million dollars)	Investment method	Industry of investor (first level)	Industry of target	Country/Region of target	Continent
2016	Alibaba Group	S.M. Entertainment	30.61	Merger and acquisition	Information transmission, computer service and software	Culture, sport and entertainment	Korea	Asia
2016	Bliss Media Ltd.	Insiders		Merger and acquisition	Culture, sport and entertainment	Culture, sport and entertainment	USA	North America
2016	Wanda Group	E-Land Group		Newly-established	Comprehensive	Culture, sporting and entertainment	Korea	Asia
2016	China Cinda Asset Management Co., Ltd.	Nanyang Commercial Bank	8767.61	Merger and acquisition	Financial	Financial	Hong Kong	Asia
2016	Guangdong Orient Zirconic Industry Science and technology Co., Ltd.	Image		Merger and acquisition	Manufacturing	Mining	Australia	Oceania
2016	TAL Education Group	Knewton		Merger and acquisition	Education	Education	USA	North America
2016	China Railway Construction Corporation Limited	Infrafer	554.19	Newly-established	Construction	Construction	Algeria	Africa
2016	HNA Group (International) Company Limited	Ingram Micro	6000.00	Merger and acquisition	Comprehensive	Information transmission,computer service and software	USA	North America
2016	Greenland Holding Group Company Limited	The Britain		Newly-established	Real estate	Real estate	UK	Europe
2016	Visual China Group	Getty Images International		Merger and acquisition	Culture, sports and entertainment	Culture, sports and entertainment	USA	North America

(continued)

(continued)

Year	Investor	Counterparty	Transaction amount (million dollars)	Investment method	Industry of investor (first level)	Industry of target	Country/Region of target	Continent
2016	Hangzhou contact information technology Co., Ltd.	Razer Pte Ltd.	75.00	Merger and acquisition	Information transmission, computer service and software	Manufacturing	USA	North America
2016	Harbin Gloria Pharmaceuticals Co., Ltd.	Proteus Digital Health, Inc	40.00	Merger and acquisition	Manufacturing	Manufacturing	UK	Europe
2016	SDIC Power Holding Co., Ltd.	Repsol Nuevas Energias S.A.	262.77	Merger and acquisition	Production and supply of power, gas and water	Production and supply of power, gas and water	UK	Europe
2016	Mobvista Network Co., Ltd.	NativeX	24.50	Merger and acquisition	Information transmission, computer service and software	Information transmission,computer service and software	USA	North America
2016	China Everbright Group	SEA Holdings Limited	1300.00	Merger and acquisition	Financial	Real estate	Hong Kong	Asia
2016	Wanda Group	Auchan Group		Newly-established	Comprehensive	Culture, sport and entertainment	France	Europe
2016	NORINCO International Cooperation Ltd.	An Energy (PVT) Limited	51.57	Newly-established	Production and supply of power, gas and water	Production and supply of power, gas and water	Pakistan	Asia
2016	UniIC Semiconductors Co., Ltd.	Powertech Technology Inc.	562.98	Merger and acquisition	Manufacturing	Manufacturing	Taiwan	Asia
2016	UniIC Semiconductors Co., Ltd.	ChipMOS Technologies (Shanghai) Ltd.	345.91	Merger and acquisition	Manufacturing	Manufacturing	Taiwan	Asia
2016	Shanghai Electric Group Company Limited	Manz AG	103.95	Merger and acquisition	Manufacturing	Manufacturing	Germany	Europe
2016	China Vanke Co., Ltd.		116.00	Merger and acquisition	Real estate	Real estate	USA	North America

(continued)

(continued)

Year	Investor	Counterparty	Transaction amount (million dollars)	Investment method	Industry of investor (first level)	Industry of target	Country/Region of target	Continent
2016	Ourpalm Co., Ltd.	NHN Entertainment Corporation	196.57	Merger and acquisition	Information transmission, computer service and software	Information transmission,computer service and software	Korea	Asia
2016	Sunflower Pharmaceutical Group Co., Ltd.		1.00	Merger and acquisition	Manufacturing	Manufacturing	USA	North America
2016	Poly Developments and Holdings		60.74	Merger and acquisition	Real estate	Real estate	Australia	Oceania
2016	Jiangxi Special Electric Motor Co., Ltd.	WeierAntriebe und Energietechnik GmbH	3.07	Merger and acquisition	Manufacturing	Manufacturing	Germany	Europe
2016	LONGI Green Energy Technology Co., Ltd.	SunEdison Kuching	63.00	Merger and acquisition	Manufacturing	Manufacturing	Malaysia	Asia
2016	China Three Gorges Corporation			Newly-established	Production and supply of power, gas and water	Production and supply of power, gas and water	Myanmar	Asia
2016	Golden Concord Holdings Limited		2500.00	Newly-established	Production and supply of power, gas and water	Production and supply of power, gas and water	Djibouti	Africa
2016	Alibaba Group	Agtech, Inc.	307.89	Merger and acquisition	Information transmission, computer service and software	Culture, sports and entertainment	Hong Kong	Asia
2016	Kangdexin Composite Material Group		35.00	Merger and acquisition	Manufacturing	Manufacturing	USA	North America

(continued)

(continued)

Year	Investor	Counterparty	Transaction amount (million dollars)	Investment method	Industry of investor (first level)	Industry of target	Country/Region of target	Continent
2016	37 Interactive Entertainment	Archiact Interactive Ltd.	3.17	Merger and acquisition	Information transmission, computer service and software	Information transmission,computer service and software	Canada	North America
2016	Tibet Rhodiolapharmaceutical Holding Co., Ltd.	ASTRAZENECA AB	190.00	Merger and acquisition	Manufacturing	Manufacturing	USA	North America
2016	Shenzhen Tencent Electronic Co., Ltd.	Radiant		Merger and acquisition	Information transmission, computer service and software	Information transmission,computer service and software	USA	North America
2016	Legend Holdings Corporation	WeWork	430.00	Merger and acquisition	Financial	Leasing and business service industry	USA	North America
2016	Dalian Dayang Trands Co., Ltd.	INDOCHINO	32.35	Merger and acquisition	Manufacturing	Manufacturing	Canada	North America
2016	Dongguan Eontec Co., Ltd.	Liquidmetal Technologies,Inc.		Merger and acquisition	Manufacturing	Manufacturing	USA	North America
2016	上海宏达矿业股份有限公司	Jagex	300.00	Merger and acquisition	Manufacturing	Information transmission,computer service and software	UK	Europe
2016	西陇科学股份有限公司	Fulgent	22.56	Merger and acquisition	Manufacturing	Scientific research,technology service and geological survey	USA	North America
2016	China National Offshore Oil Corporation	Petrobras		Merger and acquisition	Manufacturing	Manufacturing	Brazil	South America

(continued)

(continued)

Year	Investor	Counterparty	Transaction amount (million dollars)	Investment method	Industry of investor (first level)	Industry of target	Country/Region of target	Continent
2016	State Power Investment Corporation	Santander Central Hispano S.A.	227.76	Merger and acquisition	Production and supply of power, gas and water	Production and supply of power, gas and water	Australia	Oceania
2016	Ping An Insurance (Group) Company	Prenetics	10.00	Merger and acquisition	Financial	Manufacturing	Hong Kong	Asia
2016	Silk Road Fund Co., Ltd.	Oao Novatek	1400.00	Merger and acquisition	Financial	Production and supply of power, gas and water	Russia	Europe
2016	Sany Group	Ethiopian government		Newly-established	Financial	Manufacturing	Ethiopia	Africa
2016	Huayi Brothers International Limited	SIMCom Wireless Solutions	20.01	Merger and acquisition	Culture, sport and entertainment	Culture, sport and entertainment	Korea	Asia
2016	GCL System Integration Technology Co., Ltd.	ONE STOP WAREHOUSE PTY Ltd.	7.43	Merger and acquisition	Manufacturing	Wholesale and retail	Australia	Oceania
2016	Sinosteel Corporation	Empresa Siderúrgica del Mutún	450.00	Newly-established	Manufacturing	Manufacturing	Bolivia	South America
2016	CECEP Valiant Co., Ltd.	MP Biomedicals, LLC	158.57	Merger and acquisition	Manufacturing	Manufacturing	USA	North America
2016	China Post Group Corporation	Royal Bank of Scotland		Merger and acquisition	Transportation, storage and post	Financial	UK	Europe
2016	Yifan Pharmaceutical Co., Ltd.	DHY & Co., Ltd.	147.83	Merger and acquisition	Manufacturing	Manufacturing	The British Virgin Islands	North America
2016	Sincetimes HK Science Company Limited	Cowon Systems	18.32	Merger and acquisition	Information transmission, computer service and software	Manufacturing	Korea	Asia
2016	China Huiyuan Juice Group Ltd.	Yeo Hiap Seng Ltd.		Newly-established	Manufacturing	Manufacturing	Malaysia	Asia

(continued)

(continued)

Year	Investor	Counterparty	Transaction amount (million dollars)	Investment method	Industry of investor (first level)	Industry of target	Country/Region of target	Continent
2016	Pengxin Group Co., Ltd.	Metals Trading Corp.		Merger and acquisition	Mining	Mining	USA	North America
2016	Geo-Jade Petroleum Corparation	Bankers Petroleum	442.34	Merger and acquisition	Mining	Mining	Canada	North America
2016	The National Silicon Industry Group	Soitec		Merger and acquisition	Financial	Manufacturing	France	Europe
2016	YOOZOO Games Co., Ltd.	Bigpoint HoldCo GmbH	80.00	Merger and acquisition	Information transmission, computer service and software	Information transmission,computer service and software	Germany	Europe
2016	CMC Inc.	SoccerWorld	400.00	Merger and acquisition	Culture, sport and entertainment	Culture, sport and entertainment	UK	Europe
2016	CTCI Corporation	Green Motion	12.30	Merger and acquisition	Manufacturing	Manufacturing	Switzerland	Europe
2016	Huayi Brothers International Limited	HB Entertainment Co., Ltd.	35.29	Merger and acquisition	Culture, sport and entertainment	Culture, sport and entertainment	Korea	Asia
2016	Cenbest (Hong Kong) Company Limited	A.S. Nursing & Welfare Ltd.		Merger and acquisition	Wholesale and retail	Health, social security and social welfare	Israel	Asia
2016	China General Nuclear Power Group	1Malaysia Development Berhad	2300.00	Merger and acquisition	Production and supply of power, gas and water	Production and supply of power, gas and water	Malaysia	Asia
2016	ENN Energy Holdings Limited	Santos Ltd.	750.00	Merger and acquisition	Production and supply of power, gas and water	Production and supply of power, gas and water	Australia	Oceania
2016	Hony Capital	Santos Ltd.	378.89	Merger and acquisition	Financial	Production and supply of power, gas and water	Australia	Oceania

(continued)

(continued)

Year	Investor	Counterparty	Transaction amount (million dollars)	Investment method	Industry of investor (first level)	Industry of target	Country/Region of target	Continent
2016	China Railway Construction Corporation Limited	Malaysia	2000.00	Newly-established	Construction	Real estate	Malaysia	Asia
2016	Sinochem International Corporation	Halcyon AgriCoration Limited	178.81	Merger and acquisition	Leasing and business service industry	Manufacturing	Singapore	Asia
2016	China CEFC Energy Company Limited	J&T	1658.01	Merger and acquisition	Financial	Financial	Czech Republic	Europe
2016	Beijing J&E Point		40.00	Merger and acquisition	Lodging and catering	Real estate	USA	North America
2016	Shanghai Spring International Travel Services, Ltd.	Xymax corporation		Newly-established	Leasing and business service industry	Lodging and catering	Japan	Asia
2016	China Ocean Shipping(Group) Company	PSA International Pte Ltd.		Newly-established	Transportation, storage and post	Transportation, storage and post	Singapore	Asia
2016	Tahoe Group	Alliance Healthcare Services, Inc.		Merger and acquisition	Financial	Health, social security and social welfare	USA	North America
2016	Sharing Mobile	GiCell	200.00	Merger and acquisition	Information transmission, computer service and software	Information transmission,computer service and software	Nigeria	Africa
2016	Carnival Film & Television Limited	Walt Disney studio	500.00	Merger and acquisition	Culture, sport and entertainment	Culture, sport and entertainment	USA	North America
2016	Zhejiang Double Arrow Rubber Co., Ltd.	International Conveyor Products Pty Limited	1.88	Merger and acquisition	Manufacturing	Manufacturing	Australia	Oceania
2016	Humanwell Healthcare (Group) Co.	Pharma	529.00	Merger and acquisition	Manufacturing	Manufacturing	USA	North America

(continued)

(continued)

Year	Investor	Counterparty	Transaction amount (million dollars)	Investment method	Industry of investor (first level)	Industry of target	Country/Region of target	Continent
2016	Humanwell Healthcare (Group) Co.	RE Holdco	21.00	Merger and acquisition	Manufacturing	Manufacturing	USA	North America
2016	Shandong Ruyi group	SMCP	1485.77	Merger and acquisition	Manufacturing	Manufacturing	France	Europe
2016	Citychamp Dartong Co., Ltd.		46.98	Merger and acquisition	Manufacturing	Lodging and catering	Switzerland	Europe
2016	Hangzhou Yong sheng holdings Co., Ltd.	Desseilles Laces SAS	0.62	Merger and acquisition	Financial	Manufacturing	France	Europe
2016	Beijing Xiaomi Technology Co., Ltd.	Hungama	25.00	Merger and acquisition	Manufacturing	Information transmission,computer service and software	India	Asia
2016	Dr. Peng Group		15.00	Merger and acquisition	Information transmission, computer service and software	Information transmission,computer service and software	USA	North America
2016	Genimous Technology Co., Ltd.	Spigot	251.70	Merger and acquisition	Financial	Information transmission,computer service and software	USA	North America
2016	China TravelSky Holding Company Limited	OpenJaw Technologies	39.40	Merger and acquisition	Transportation, storage and post	Leasing and business service industry	Ireland	Europe
2016	Greatoo Intelligent Equipment Inc.	OPS Holding	11.24	Merger and acquisition	Manufacturing	Manufacturing	Germany	Europe
2016	HNA Group (International) Company Limited	Shorenstein Realty Service	463.00	Merger and acquisition	Comprehensive	Real estate	USA	North America

(continued)

(continued)

Year	Investor	Counterparty	Transaction amount (million dollars)	Investment method	Industry of investor (first level)	Industry of target	Country/Region of target	Continent
2016	Invengo Information Technology Co., Ltd.	TAGSYS	6.82	Merger and acquisition	Information transmission, computer service and software	Manufacturing	France	Europe
2016	Anbang Insurance Group	Allianz Life, South Korea subsidiary	216.22	Merger and acquisition	Financial	Financial	Korea	Asia
2016	Shenzhen Selen Science & Technology Co., Ltd.	T&T Enertechno	84.93	Merger and acquisition	Manufacturing	Manufacturing	Japan	Asia
2016	Legend Holdings Corporation	Kailis	722.13	Newly-established	Financial	Agriculture, forestry, animal husbandry and fishing	Australia	Oceania
2016	China Construction Bank	Metdist Trading Limited		Merger and acquisition	Financial	Financial	UK	Europe
2016	Jangho Group Company Limited	Primary Health Care Limited	201.78	Merger and acquisition	Construction	Health, social security and social welfare	Australia	Oceania
2016	Alibaba Group	Skydance Media		Newly-established	Culture, sport and entertainment	Culture, sport and entertainment	USA	North America
2016	Zhejiang Hailiang Co., Ltd.	JMF Company	30.00	Merger and acquisition	Manufacturing	Manufacturing	USA	North America
2016	Kingenta Ecological Engineering Group Co., Ltd.	Compo AcquiCo S.à.r.l.	130.46	Merger and acquisition	Manufacturing	Irrigation, environment and infrastructure management	Luxembourg Germany France	Europe
2016	Nanjing Aotecar New Energy Technology Co., Ltd.	Air International Thermal Systems	135.00	Merger and acquisition	Manufacturing	Manufacturing	Australia	Oceania
2016	Zhuhai Zhen Rong Company	Myanmar	3000.00	Newly-established	Manufacturing	Manufacturing	Myanmar	Asia

(continued)

(continued)

Year	Investor	Counterparty	Transaction amount (million dollars)	Investment method	Industry of investor (first level)	Industry of target	Country/Region of target	Continent
2016	HNA Group (International) Company Limited	Chia Meei Food Indl. Corp.	1462.46	Merger and acquisition	Comprehensive	Lodging and catering	Switzerland	Europe
2016	Zhejiang Kaishan Compressor Co., Ltd.	OTP Geothermal Pte., Ltd.	60.00	Merger and acquisition	Manufacturing	Manufacturing	Singapore	Asia
2016	Huatai Securities Company Limited	AssetMark Financial Holdings, Inc.	780.00	Merger and acquisition	Financial	Financial	USA	North America
2016	HNA Group (International) Company Limited	Mazaya		Merger and acquisition	Comprehensive	Financial	Saudi Arabia	Asia
2016	Alibaba Group	Lazada Group SA	1000	Merger and acquisition	Information transmission, computer service and software	Information transmission,computer service and software	Singapore	Asia
2016	Qingdao Sentury Tire Co., Ltd.	立盛橡胶工业园	103.06	Merger and acquisition	Manufacturing	Manufacturing	Thailand	Asia
2016	Shanda Group	Trian Fund Management LP	340.00	Merger and acquisition	Comprehensive	Financial	USA	North America
2016	Shanghai Kaichuang Marine Int'l Co., Ltd.	Hijos De Carlos Albo S.l.	69.77	Merger and acquisition	Agriculture, forestry, animal husbandry and fishing	Manufacturing	Spain	Europe
2016	Anbang Insurance Group	Strategic Hotels & Resorts Inc	6500.00	Merger and acquisition	Financial	Lodging and catering	USA	North America
2016	HAERS Co., Ltd.	SIGG Switzerland Bottles AG	16.83	Merger and acquisition	Manufacturing	Manufacturing	Switzerland	Europe
2016	Shimge Pump Industry Group Co., Ltd.	WITA Wilhelm Taake GmbH	6.21	Merger and acquisition	Manufacturing	Manufacturing	Germany	Europe

(continued)

(continued)

Year	Investor	Counterparty	Transaction amount (million dollars)	Investment method	Industry of investor (first level)	Industry of target	Country/Region of target	Continent
2016	Shimge Pump Industry Group Co., Ltd.	HEL-WITA Sp. z o.o.	6.55	Merger and acquisition	Manufacturing	Manufacturing	Poland	Europe
2016	Shimge Pump Industry Group Co., Ltd.		2.48	Merger and acquisition	Manufacturing	Real estate	Germany	Europe
2016	HNA Group (International) Company Limited	International Currency Exchange		Merger and acquisition	Comprehensive	Financial	UK	Europe
2016	Hebei Hengxin Mobile Business Company Limited	Virtual Reality Company	22.70	Merger and acquisition	Information transmission, computer service and software	Culture, sports and entertainment	USA	North America
2016	LingLong Americas, Inc.		700.00	Newly-established	Manufacturing	Manufacturing	Thailand	Asia
2016	China Minsheng Investment Co., Ltd.	Sirius International Insurance Group	2500.00	Merger and acquisition	Financial	Financial	UK	Europe
2016	CITIC CAPITAL	Biosensors International Group Limited	1050.00	Merger and acquisition	Financial	Manufacturing	Singapore	Asia
2016	Tsinghua Unigroup Ltd.	Lattice Semiconductor, LSCC	41.60	Merger and acquisition	Manufacturing	Manufacturing	USA	North America
2016	HNA Group (International) Company Limited	Tysan Holdings Limited	337.07	Merger and acquisition	Comprehensive	Construction	Hong Kong	Asia
2016	Zhonghong Holding Co., Ltd.	KEE Holdings Company Limited	90.25	Merger and acquisition	Real estate	Manufacturing	Hong Kong	Asia
2016	AVIC International Holding Corporation	AritexCading, S.A		Merger and acquisition	Comprehensive	Manufacturing	Spain	Europe
2016	黑龙江省时嘉国际贸易集团有限公司	Komi Republic	100.00	Newly-established	Manufacturing	Comprehensive	Russia	Europe

(continued)

(continued)

Year	Investor	Counterparty	Transaction amount (million dollars)	Investment method	Industry of investor (first level)	Industry of target	Country/Region of target	Continent
2016	China Life Insurance (Group) Company		506.61	Merger and acquisition	Financial	Real estate	UK	Europe
2016	Guangdong Dynavolt Power Technology Co., Ltd.		6.85	Merger and acquisition	Manufacturing	Manufacturing	Switzerland	Europe
2016	HNA Group (International) Company Limited			Merger and acquisition	Comprehensive	Lodging and catering	USA	North America
2016	ELLASSAY Co., Ltd.	唐利国际	35.51	Merger and acquisition	Manufacturing	Manufacturing	Hong Kong	Asia
2016	Ping An Insurance (Group) Company of China, Ltd.	Private equity 3i	175.62	Merger and acquisition	Financial	Manufacturing	UK	Europe
2016	Beyondsoft Corporation		1.85	Merger and acquisition	Information transmission, computer service and software	Information transmission,computer service and software	USA	North America
2016	China Mengniu Dairy Company Limited		220.08	Merger and acquisition	Manufacturing	Manufacturing	Australia	Oceania
2016	Sinocare International Limited	Polymer Technology Systems, Inc.和Shareholder Representative Services LLC	110.00	Merger and acquisition	Manufacturing	Manufacturing	USA	North America
2016	Ningbo Joyson Electronic Corp	EVANA	19.50	Merger and acquisition	Manufacturing	Manufacturing	USA	North America

(continued)

(continued)

Year	Investor	Counterparty	Transaction amount (million dollars)	Investment method	Industry of investor (first level)	Industry of target	Country/Region of target	Continent
2016	Envision Energy International Limited	BazeField		Merger and acquisition	Scientific research, technology service and geological survey	Scientific research, technology service and geological survey	Norway	Europe
2016	Legend Holdings Corporation	Pension Insurance Corporation,PIC	142.92	Merger and acquisition	Financial	Financial	UK	Europe
2016	Guangdong Alpha Animation and Culture Co., Ltd.	Kadokawa Games Ltd.	0.10	Merger and acquisition	Culture, sports and entertainment	Culture, sports and entertainment	Japan	Asia
2016	Tsinghua Unigroup Ltd.	Imagination Technologies		Merger and acquisition	Manufacturing	Manufacturing	UK	Europe
2016	China Molybdenum Co., Ltd.	Freeport-McMoRan Inc.	2650.00	Merger and acquisition	Manufacturing	Mining	Congo	Africa
2016	Techmation Electric & Controls Ltd.		6.97	Merger and acquisition	Manufacturing	Manufacturing	Italy	Europe
2016	China Construction Bank	Oaktree Capital Management		Merger and acquisition	Financial	Manufacturing	France	Europe
2016	COSCO Pacific Limited	ECT Participations	140.85	Merger and acquisition	Transportation, storage and post	Transportation, storage and post	Holland	Europe
2016	Wanda Group	Odeon&UCI Cinemas Group		Merger and acquisition	Comprehensive	Culture, sport and entertainment	UK	Europe
2016	CMC Holdings	Cityneon Holdings Limited		Merger and acquisition	Culture, sport and entertainment	Culture, sport and entertainment	Singapore	Asia
2016	Wanda Group	Propaganda GEM		Merger and acquisition	Comprehensive	Culture, sport and entertainment	USA	North America

(continued)

(continued)

Year	Investor	Counterparty	Transaction amount (million dollars)	Investment method	Industry of investor (first level)	Industry of target	Country/Region of target	Continent
2016	Tsinghua Holdings Capital	Marvell Technology Group Ltd.		Merger and acquisition	Financial	Manufacturing	USA	North America
2016	Industrial and Commercial Bank of China	BARC.L		Merger and acquisition	Financial	Financial	UK	Europe
2016	MLS Co., Ltd.	OSRAM GmbH.		Merger and acquisition	Manufacturing	Manufacturing	Germany	Europe
2016	China Vanke Co., Ltd.	Laconia Development		Newly-established	Real estate	Real estate	USA	North America
2016	Changchun Sinoenergy Corporation	Long Run	601.24	Merger and acquisition	Production and supply of power, gas and water	Mining	Canada	North America
2016	Chong Sing Holdings FinTech Group Limited	Amigo Technologies Joint Stock Company	12.72	Merger and acquisition	Financial	Financial	Vietnam	Asia
2016	Guangdong Dongfang Precision Science & Technology Co., Ltd.	EDF Europe S.R.L.	10.61	Merger and acquisition	Manufacturing	Manufacturing	Italy	Europe
2016	Daohe Sports			Merger and acquisition	Culture, sport and entertainment	Culture, sport and entertainment	Italy	Europe
2016	Hangzhou Hikvision Digital Technology Co., Ltd.	Secure Holdings Limited		Merger and acquisition	Manufacturing	Manufacturing	UK	Europe
2016	Qingjian Group Co., Ltd.		463.46	Merger and acquisition	Construction	Real estate	Singapore	Asia
2016	Zhejiang Yinlun Machinery Co., Ltd.			Merger and acquisition	Manufacturing	Manufacturing	USA	North America
2016	Shanda Group	Lending Club		Merger and acquisition	Comprehensive	Financial	USA	North America

(continued)

(continued)

Year	Investor	Counterparty	Transaction amount (million dollars)	Investment method	Industry of investor (first level)	Industry of target	Country/Region of target	Continent
2016	上海浸鑫投资咨询合伙企业	MP & Silva		Merger and acquisition	Financial	Culture, sport and entertainment	UK	Europe
2016	Zhejiang Chimin Pharmaceutical Co., Ltd.	Linear Chemicals S.L.	5.59	Merger and acquisition	Manufacturing	Manufacturing	Spain	Europe
2016	Zhongding Group	AMK	139.41	Merger and acquisition	Manufacturing	Manufacturing	Germany	Europe
2016	LandBridge Group			Merger and acquisition	Comprehensive	Transportation, storage and post	Panama	South America
2016	Anbang Insurance Group	GWL Realty Advisors Inc.	508.16	Merger and acquisition	Financial	Real estate	Canada	North America
2016	Join In (Holding) Co., Ltd.	EyeSight	15.00	Merger and acquisition	Real estate	Scientific research, technology service and geological survey	Israel	Asia
2016	SDIC Power Holdings Co., Ltd.	WFEUK(Wind Farm Energy UK Limited)	268.40	Merger and acquisition	Production and supply of power, gas and water	Production and supply of power, gas and water	UK	Europe
2016	Qingjian Group Co., Ltd.	New Chic International Limited	73.52	Merger and acquisition	Construction	Construction	Singapore	Asia
2016	HNA Group (International) Company Limited	TAP Portugal Airline		Merger and acquisition	Transportation, storage and post	Transportation, storage and post	Portugal	Europe
2016	China Life Insurance (Group) Company		1650.00	Merger and acquisition	Financial	Real estate	USA	North America
2016	Beijing Weying Technology Co. Ltd.	YG Entertainment	55.00	Merger and acquisition	Culture, sport and entertainment	Culture, sport and entertainment	Korea	Asia

(continued)

(continued)

Year	Investor	Counterparty	Transaction amount (million dollars)	Investment method	Industry of investor (first level)	Industry of target	Country/Region of target	Continent
2016	Tencent Technology (shenzhen) Company Limited	YG Entertainment	30.00	Merger and acquisition	Information transmission, computer service and software	Culture, sport and entertainment	Korea	Asia
2016	Creat Group Corporation	Bain Capital LLC and UK Department of Health	1197.00	Merger and acquisition	Comprehensive	Manufacturing	UK	Europe
2016	Shanda Group	Sotheby's		Merger and acquisition	Comprehensive	Financial	UK	Europe
2016	Shanghai Yuyuan Tourist Mart Company Limited	Hoshino Resorts Tomamu	142.62	Merger and acquisition	Leasing and business service industry	Lodging and catering	Japan	Asia
2016	Midea Group	KUKA Aktiengesellschaft	4397.00	Merger and acquisition	Manufacturing	Manufacturing	Germany	Europe
2016	China National Chemical Corporation	SGL Carbon SE		Merger and acquisition	Manufacturing	Manufacturing	Germany	Europe
2016	HNA Group (International) Company Limited	Virgin Australia Holdings Ltd. (VAH.AU)	112.95	Merger and acquisition	Comprehensive	Transportation, storage and post	Australia	Oceania
2016	HNA Group (International) Company Limited	Air France		Merger and acquisition	Comprehensive	Transportation, storage and post	France	Europe
2016	China Cinda Asset Management Co., Ltd.	Nanyang Commercial Bank		Merger and acquisition	Financial	Financial	Hong Kong	Asia
2016	Xiwang Group	Iovate Health Sciences International Inc	730.00	Merger and acquisition	Manufacturing	Manufacturing	Canada	North America

(continued)

(continued)

Year	Investor	Counterparty	Transaction amount (million dollars)	Investment method	Industry of investor (first level)	Industry of target	Country/Region of target	Continent
2016	Alibaba Group	Twiggle	5.30	Merger and acquisition	Information transmission, computer service and software	Information transmission,computer service and software	Israel	Asia
2016	Ping An Real Estate	Mirvac Group		Newly-established	Real estate	Real estate	Australia	Oceania
2016	Tahoe Group	Dah Sing Financial Holdings Ltd.	1366.00	Merger and acquisition	Financial	Financial	Hong Kong	Asia
2016	State Grid Corporation of China	Belgian Power Grid Corpration Eandis		Merger and acquisition	Production and supply of power, gas and water	Production and supply of power, gas and water	Belgium	Europe
2016	China International Marine Containers (Group) Co., Ltd.	Briggs	33.25	Merger and acquisition	Manufacturing	Manufacturing	UK	Europe
2016	Zhejiang Vie Science and Technology Co., Ltd.	Protean Holdings Corp.	20.00	Merger and acquisition	Manufacturing	Manufacturing	USA	North America
2016	Fosun Group	Compagnie des Alpes		Merger and acquisition	Comprehensive	Leasing and business service industry	France	Europe
2016	Starway Bio-Technology Co., Ltd.	Global Systems Limited	11.00	Merger and acquisition	Manufacturing	Manufacturing	Hong Kong	Asia
2016	AVIC International Holding Corporation	AIM Altitude		Merger and acquisition	Comprehensive	Manufacturing	UK	Europe
2016	Zhongding Group	AMK Holding GmbH & Co. KG	145.68	Merger and acquisition	Manufacturing	Manufacturing	Germany	Europe
2016	Pengxin Group Co., Ltd.	Banco Indusval & Partners SA (BI&P)	3000.00	Merger and acquisition	Comprehensive	Financial	Brazil	South America
2016	Jiangsu Tongguang Optical Fiber Cable Co., Ltd.	Advait Infratech Pvt. Ltd.	3.28	Newly-established	Manufacturing	Manufacturing	India	Asia

(continued)

(continued)

Year	Investor	Counterparty	Transaction amount (million dollars)	Investment method	Industry of investor (first level)	Industry of target	Country/Region of target	Continent
2016	China Three Gorges Corporation	Blackstone Group	1805.76	Merger and acquisition	Production and supply of power, gas and water	Production and supply of power, gas and water	Germany	Europe
2016	Nanshan Group	Air New Zealand	145.00	Merger and acquisition	Comprehensive	Transportation, storage and post	Australia	Oceania
2016	Spearhead IMC Group	Smaato	148.00	Merger and acquisition	Culture, sport and entertainment	Culture, sport and entertainment	USA	North America
2016	Asia Innovations Group Limited	MimiCam		Merger and acquisition	Information transmission, computer service and software	Information transmission,computer service and software	Taiwan	Asia
2016	China Orient Summit Capital Co., Ltd.	Portman Holdings	217.00	Merger and acquisition	Real estate	Real estate	USA	North America
2016	JAC Ccpital	NXP Semiconductors	2750.00	Merger and acquisition	Financial	Manufacturing	Holland	Europe
2016	AGIC Capital	Gimatic	113.00	Merger and acquisition	financial	Manufacturing	Italy	Europe
2016	Fosun Group	Greece government		Newly-established	Comprehensive	Transportation, storage and post	Greece	Europe
2016	DeTai New Energy Group Limited	Emission Particle Solution Sweden AB		Merger and acquisition	Manufacturing	Wholesale and retail	Switzerland	Europe
2016	Tencent Technology (shenzhen) Company Limited	IM Global		Merger and acquisition	Information transmission, computer service and software	Culture, sport and entertainment	USA	North America

(continued)

(continued)

Year	Investor	Counterparty	Transaction amount (million dollars)	Investment method	Industry of investor (first level)	Industry of target	Country/Region of target	Continent
2016	Desports	Italian Pozzo Family	42.22	Merger and acquisition	Culture, sport and entertainment	Culture, sport and entertainment	Spain	Europe
2016	Nanjidianshang Group	Cartelo Crocodile Pte Ltd.	89.60	Merger and acquisition	Comprehensive	Manufacturing	Singapore	Asia
2016	MLS Co., Ltd.		47.53	Merger and acquisition	Manufacturing	Manufacturing	Hong Kong	Asia
2016	HNA Group (International) Company Limited	Fourteen Ninety Two Limited	189.00	Merger and acquisition	Comprehensive	Real estate	UK	Europe
2016	Shenzhen Hepalink Pharmaceutical Group Co., Ltd.	TPG Biotechnology Partners V, L.P.	60.00	Merger and acquisition	Manufacturing	Manufacturing	USA	North America
2016	Shanda Group	Lumus		Merger and acquisition	Comprehensive	Manufacturing	Israel	Asia
2016	Zhejiang Crystal-Optech Co., Ltd.	Lumus		Merger and acquisition	Manufacturing	Manufacturing	Israel	Asia
2016	Hejing Culture	Ingenious Media	200.00	Merger and acquisition	Culture, sports and entertainment	Culture, sport and entertainment	UK	Europe
2016	Shanda Group	LendingClub	160	Merger and acquisition	Comprehensive	Financial	USA	North America
2016	Shanghai Runda Medical Technology Co., Ltd.	Response Biomedical Corp.	6.00	Merger and acquisition	Manufacturing	Manufacturing	Canada	North America
2016	LeTV	Yahoo!	250.00	Merger and acquisition	Culture, sport and entertainment	Real estate	USA	North America
2016	Ant financial services group	Ascend Money		Merger and acquisition	Financial	Financial	Thailand	Asia

(continued)

(continued)

Year	Investor	Counterparty	Transaction amount (million dollars)	Investment method	Industry of investor (first level)	Industry of target	Country/Region of target	Continent
2016	Anbang Insurance Group	Woori Bank	300.00	Merger and acquisition	Financial	Financial	Korea	Asia
2016	Fosun Group	俄罗斯中央军事百货商场	169.40	Merger and acquisition	Comprehensive	Real estate	Russia	Europe
2016	JSTI Group	TestAmerica ENVIRONMENTAL SERVICES LLC		Merger and acquisition	Construction	Irrigation, environment and infrastructure management	USA	North America
2016	Tianjin Keyvia Electric Co., Ltd.	Balfour Beatty Rail GmbH, BICC Holdings GmbH	14.85	Merger and acquisition	Manufacturing	Manufacturing	Germany	Europe
2016	Zhejiang Fuchunjiang Hydropower Equipment Co., Ltd.	PT Dharma Hydro Nusantara	57.74	Merger and acquisition	Manufacturing	Production and supply of power, gas and water	Indonesia	Asia
2016	Baidu, Inc.	Circle Internet Financial		Merger and acquisition	Information transmission, computer service and software	Information transmission,computer service and software	USA	North America
2016	Haier Group	Industrial park in Pune, Maharashtra, India		Newly-established	Manufacturing	Manufacturing	India	Asia
2016	Fosun Group	GUESS?, Inc.		Merger and acquisition	Comprehensive	Manufacturing	France	Europe
2016	Ningbo MedicalSystem Biotechnology Co., Ltd.	Atherotech Inc.	19.60	Merger and acquisition	Manufacturing	Scientific research, technology service and geological survey	USA	North America
2016	COL Digital Publishing Group Co., Ltd.	Joingear Limited	8.60	Merger and acquisition	Education	Education	UK	Europe
2016	Semiconductor Manufacturing International Corporation	LFoundry Europe GmbH, Marsica Innovation S.p.A.	55.91	Merger and acquisition	Manufacturing	Manufacturing	Italy	Europe

(continued)

(continued)

Year	Investor	Counterparty	Transaction amount (million dollars)	Investment method	Industry of investor (first level)	Industry of target	Country/Region of target	Continent
2016	Midea Group	Clivet Aircon Limited		Merger and acquisition	Manufacturing	Manufacturing	Italy	Europe
2016	Camel Group Co., Ltd.	SC Uzavtosnoat		Merger and acquisition	Leasing and business service industry	Manufacturing	Uzbekistan	Asia
2016	STATE GRID Corporation of China	Camargo CorreaSA		Merger and acquisition	Production and supply of power, gas and water	Production and supply of power, gas and water	Brazil	South America
2016	Desports	NBA		Merger and acquisition	Culture, sport and entertainment	Culture, sport and entertainment	USA	North America
2016	Petrotech Inc.	Three natural persons of American nationality	22.50	Merger and acquisition	Scientific research, technology service and geological survey	Scientific research, technology service and geological survey	USA	North America
2016	Beijing Enterprises Group Company Limited	Rosneft Oil		Merger and acquisition	Financial	Mining	Russia	Europe
2016	Northern Heavy Industry Group	The Robbins Company		Merger and acquisition	Manufacturing	Manufacturing	USA	North America
2016	Greenleaf Sci. & Tech. Group	Lifecode Inc.		Merger and acquisition	Health, social security and social welfare	Health, social security and social welfare	USA	North America
2016	Shenghe Resources Holding Co., Ltd.	Vietnam Rare Earth Company Limited		Merger and acquisition	Manufacturing	Manufacturing	Vietnam	Asia
2016	China International Marine Containers (Group) Co., Ltd.	Retlan Manufacturing Limited	121.99	Merger and acquisition	Manufacturing	Manufacturing	UK	Europe

(continued)

(continued)

Year	Investor	Counterparty	Transaction amount (million dollars)	Investment method	Industry of investor (first level)	Industry of target	Country/Region of target	Continent
2016	Andon Health Company Limited	eDevice	105.20	Merger and acquisition	Manufacturing	Information transmission,computer service and software	France	Europe
2016	Shanghai Maling Aquarius Co., Ltd.	Silver Fern Farms	187.00	Merger and acquisition	Manufacturing	Manufacturing	New Zealand	Oceania
2016	Citic Guoan Information Industry Co., Ltd.	NextVR Inc.	20.00	Merger and acquisition	Information transmission, computer service and software	Information transmission,computer service and software	USA	North America
2016	Greenland Holding Group Company Limited	Golden Horse		Newly-established	real estate	real estate	Australia	Oceania
2016	Cenbest (Hong Kong) Company Limited	Wells Spring Pte Ltd., Providence Investment Pte Ltd. 和Coop International Pte Ltd.	64.64	Newly-established	Manufacturing	Manufacturing	Singapore	Asia
2016	Midea Group	Toshiba Corporation	458.68	Merger and acquisition	Manufacturing	manufactuRING	Japan	Asia
2016	Sunward Equipment Group	Avmax Group Inc.	116.00	Merger and acquisition	Manufacturing	Leasing and business service industry	Canada	North America
2016	China Ocean Shipping(Group) Company	Port of Piraeus	368.50	Merger and acquisition	Transportation, storage and post	Transportation, storage and post	Greece	Europe
2016	Lenovo Group	NEC Corporation	195.00	Merger and acquisition	Manufacturing	Manufacturing	Japan	Asia
2016	Shanghai Hongda Mining Co., Ltd.	Jagex Ltd.		Merger and acquisition	Mining	Information Transmission, computer service and software	UK	Europe
2016	ESR Cayman Limited	Higashi Ogijima		Newly-established	Real estate	Real estate	Japan	Asia

(continued)

(continued)

Year	Investor	Counterparty	Transaction amount (million dollars)	Investment method	Industry of investor (first level)	Industry of target	Country/Region of target	Continent
2016	Xinjiang Hualing Industry & Trade (Group) Co., Ltd.	Societe Generale Group		Merger and acquisition	Comprehensive	Financial	Georgia	Asia
2016	Tencent Technology (Shenzhen) Company Limited	Supercell	8600.00	Merger and acquisition	Information transmission, computer service and software	Information transmission, computer service and software	Finland	Europe
2016	Zhejiang Kaishan Compressor Co., Ltd.	Turawell Geothermal Project in Hungary	2.24	Merger and acquisition	Manufacturing	Production and supply of power, gas and water	Hungary	Europe
2016	Zhejiang Fuchunjiang Hydropower Equipment Co., Ltd.		1668.00	Newly-established	Manufacturing	Production and supply of power, gas and water	Indonesia	Asia
2016	Tianjin Bohai Leasing Co., Ltd.	GECAS	1970.00	Merger and acquisition	Leasing and business service industry	Leasing and business service industry	USA	North America
2016	Ledman Optoelectronic Co., Ltd.	Newcastle Jets Football Club		Merger and acquisition	Manufacturing	Culture, sport and entertainment	Australia	Oceania
2016	Chengdu Techcent Environment Co., Ltd.	Chengdu Zhongde Tianxiang Investment Co., Ltd.	250.82	Merger and acquisition	Irrigation, environment and infrastructure management	Irrigation, environment and infrastructure management	Germany	Europe
2016	Ningbo MedicalSystem Biotechnology Co., Ltd.	Kyoto Life Sciences Co.	0.18	Merger and acquisition	Manufacturing	Manufacturing	Japan	Asia
2016	Guangdong Dongfang Precision Science & Technology Co., Ltd.	EDF EUROPE S.R.L.	10.59	Merger and acquisition	Manufacturing	Manufacturing	Italy	Europe
2016	Zhejiang Huahai Pharmaceutical Co., Ltd.	Vivo Panda Fund,L.P	10.00	Merger and acquisition	Manufacturing	Financial	USA	North America

(continued)

(continued)

Year	Investor	Counterparty	Transaction amount (million dollars)	Investment method	Industry of investor (first level)	Industry of target	Country/Region of target	Continent
2016	Leyou Technologies Holdings Limited	Splash Damage	150.00	Merger and acquisition	Information transmission, computer service and software	Information transmission, computer service and software	UK	Europe
2016	Hunan Dakang International Food & Agriculture Co., Ltd.	Fiagril Ltda.	200.00	Merger and acquisition	Agriculture, forestry, animal husbandry and fishing	Agriculture, forestry, animal husbandry and fishing	Brazil	South America
2016	Fortune Ng Fung Food (Hebei) Co., Ltd.	Glenbrae and Leumeah farms in Australia	5.37	Merger and acquisition	Agriculture, forestry, animal husbandry and fishing	Agriculture, forestry, animal husbandry and fishing	Australia	Oceania
2016	Shanghai Kaichuang Marine Int'l Co., Ltd.	Hijos de Carlos Albo, S.L.	68.36	Merger and acquisition	Agriculture, forestry, animal husbandry and fishing	Agriculture, forestry, animal husbandry and fishing	Spain	Europe
2016	Wei Long Grape Wine Co., Ltd.		9.21	Newly-established	Manufacturing	Manufacturing	Australia	Oceania
2016	Shenzhen Selen Science & Technology Co., Ltd.	Toppan Printing Co. Ltd., Toyo Seikan and T&T Enertechno	93.98	Merger and acquisition	Manufacturing	Manufacturing	Japan	Asia
2016	Meinian Onehealth Healthcare (Group) Co., Ltd.	Xin Xin Healthcare Holding Limited	27.19	Merger and acquisition	Health, social security and social welfare	Health, social security and social welfare	Taiwan	Asia
2016	Kingenta Ecological Engineering Group Co., Ltd.	Compo AcquiCo S.à.r.l.	129.99	Merger and acquisition	Manufacturing	Agriculture, forestry, animal husbandry and fishing	Luxembourg	Europe

(continued)

(continued)

Year	Investor	Counterparty	Transaction amount (million dollars)	Investment method	Industry of investor (first level)	Industry of target	Country/Region of target	Continent
2016	Mobvista Network Co., Ltd.	GameAnalytics	11.72	Merger and acquisition	Information transmission, computer service and software	Information transmission, computer service and software	Denmark	Europe
2016	HNA Group (International) Company Limited	Mubadala Development Company		Merger and acquisition	Comprehensive	Transportation, storage and post	Switzerland	Europe
2016	China Railway Construction Corporation Limited			Newly-established	Construction	Construction	India	Asia
2016	Weichai Power Co., Ltd.	KION Group	309.29	Merger and acquisition	Manufacturing	Manufacturing	Germany	Europe
2016	Boai NKY Pharmaceuticals Ltd.	Navigation Dynamics AB	2.62	Merger and acquisition	Manufacturing	Health, social security and social welfare	Sweden	Europe
2016	Baidu, Inc.	ZestFinance		Merger and acquisition	Information transmission, computer service and software	Financial	USA	North America
2016	Sundiro Holding Co., Ltd.	Lorsinal S.A.	16.65		Manufacturing	Agriculture, forestry, animal husbandry and fishing	Uruguay	South America
2016	Recon Group, Inc.	Aston Villa Football Club	99.53	Merger and acquisition	Comprehensive	Culture, sport and entertainment	UK	Europe
2016	Jiuquan Iron & Steel (Group) Co., Ltd.	UC RUSAL	299.00	Merger and acquisition	Manufacturing	Manufacturing	Jamaica	South America
2016	Cheung Kei Group	Wheelock and Company Limited	688.05	Merger and acquisition	Comprehensive	Real estate	Hong Kong	Asia

(continued)

(continued)

Year	Investor	Counterparty	Transaction amount (million dollars)	Investment method	Industry of investor (first level)	Industry of target	Country/Region of target	Continent
2016	HNA Group (International) Company Limited	Azul S.A.	33.62	Merger and acquisition	Comprehensive	Transportation, storage and post	Portugal	Europe
2016	Beijing Teamsun Technology Co., Ltd.	BGV III,L.P.	3.00	Merger and acquisition	Information transmission, computer service and software	Financial	USA	North America
2016	PhiChem Corporation	APEX Process Technology,Corp.	15.06	Merger and acquisition	Manufacturing	Manufacturing	Taiwan	Asia
2016	Semiconductor Manufacturing International Corporation	LFoundry Europe and Marsica	54.91	Merger and acquisition	Manufacturing	Manufacturing	Italy	Europe
2016	Midea Group Co., Ltd.	KUKA Aktiengesellschaft		Merger and acquisition	Manufacturing	Manufacturing	Germany	Europe
2016	Sinocare Inc.	Polymer Technology Systems, Inc.	110.00	Merger and acquisition	Manufacturing	Manufacturing	USA	North America
2016	China Vanke Co., Ltd.	Blackstone Group	573.48	Merger and acquisition	Real estate	Real estate	USA	North America
2016	Jilin Zixin Pharmaceutical Industrial Co., Ltd.	Nabsys 2.0	42.00	Merger and acquisition	Manufacturing	Scientific research, technology service and geological survey	USA	North America
2016	Fosun Group	Wolverhampton Wanderers	59.87	Newly-established	Comprehensive	Culture, sports and entertainment	UK	Europe
2016	Suzhou Greenleaf Daily Commodity Co., Ltd.	Acino AG and Acino Supply AG	274.55	Merger and acquisition	Health, social security and social welfare	Health, social security and social welfare	Switzerland	Europe
2016	Wanda Group	Carmike Cinemas	1200.00	Merger and acquisition	Comprehensive	Culture, sport and entertainment	USA	North America

(continued)

(continued)

Year	Investor	Counterparty	Transaction amount (million dollars)	Investment method	Industry of investor (first level)	Industry of target	Country/Region of target	Continent
2016	Alibaba Group	M-DAQ	88.05	Merger and acquisition	Information transmission, computer service and software	Financial	Singapore	Asia
2016	ELLASSAY Co., Ltd.	IRO paris	58.36	Merger and acquisition	Manufacturing	Manufacturing	France	Europe
2016	Fosun Group	Gland Pharma	1091.00	Merger and acquisition	Comprehensive	Manufacturing	India	Asia
2016	Maple Leaf Educational Systems	Lucrum Development	49.38	Merger and acquisition	Education	Real estate	Singapore	Asia
2016	MMTec, Inc.	Whitewood Group		Merger and acquisition	Financial	Financial	USA	North America
2016	Taikang Life Insurance Co., Ltd.	Sotheby's	230.00	Merger and acquisition	financial	financial	UK	Europe
2016	Fosun Group			Newly-established	Comprehensive	Construction	UK	Europe
2016	Fosun Group	Rio Bravo Investimentos Ltd.	300.00	Merger and acquisition	Comprehensive	Financial	Brazil	South America
2016	Yunnan Water Investment Limited	Galaxy NewSpring	100.00	Merger and acquisition	Irrigation, environment and infrastructure management	Irrigation, environment and infrastructure management	Singapore	Asia
2016	Giant Interactive Group Inc.	Aesars Entertainment Corp.	4400.00	Merger and acquisition	Information transmission, computer service and software	Information transmission, computer service and software	Israel	Asia
2016	West Coast Development Group	Media Chinese International Ltd.	63.81	Merger and acquisition	Construction	Culture, sport and entertainment	Hong Kong	Asia

(continued)

(continued)

Year	Investor	Counterparty	Transaction amount (million dollars)	Investment method	Industry of investor (first level)	Industry of target	Country/Region of target	Continent
2016	Beijing Xiaoju Technology Co., Ltd.	Uber China	1000.00	Merger and acquisition	Information transmission, computer service and software	Information transmission, computer service and software	USA	North America
2016	Cheetah Mobile Inc.	News Republic	57.00	Merger and acquisition	Information transmission, computer service and software	Information transmission, computer service and software	USA	North America
2016	Safbon Water Service (Holding) inc., Shanghai	Stoll Family and Coreo AG		Merger and acquisition	Irrigation, environment and infrastructure management	Irrigation, environment and infrastructure management	Germany	Europe
2016	HNA Group (International) Company Limited	RocketSpace	336.00	Merger and acquisition	Comprehensive	Information transmission, computer service and software	USA	North America
2016	Shanghai Pharmaceuticals Holding Co., Ltd.	SIIC, Primavera Capital Group, Zeus, Vitaco	138.41	Merger and acquisition	Manufacturing	Manufacturing	Australia	Oceania
2016	Sinocare International Limited	XNUO WORLD Company	总 210.1256	Merger and acquisition	Manufacturing	Manufacturing	USA	North America
2016	Beijing Xiaoju Technology Co., Ltd.	Grab		Merger and acquisition	Information transmission, computer service and software	Information transmission, computer service and software		Asia
2016	Sichuan Yahua Industrial Group Co., Ltd.	澳大利亚民爆企业尼德鲁		Merger and acquisition	Manufacturing	Manufacturing	Australia	Oceania

(continued)

(continued)

Year	Investor	Counterparty	Transaction amount (million dollars)	Investment method	Industry of investor (first level)	Industry of target	Country/Region of target	Continent
2016	云毅国凯(上海)体育发展有限公司	West Bromwich Albion Limited	227.08	Merger and acquisition	Culture, sport and entertainment	Culture, sport and entertainment	UK	Europe
2016	Haixia Capital Management Co., Ltd.	AC Milan	总 560.73	Merger and acquisition	Financial	Culture, sport and entertainment	Italy	Europe
2016	中欧体育投资管理长兴有限公司	AC Milan	总 560.73	Merger and acquisition	Culture, sport and entertainment	Culture, sport and entertainment	Italy	Europe
2016	Development & Investment Corp., Ltd.	AC Milan	总 560.73	Merger and acquisition	Financial	Culture, sport and entertainment	Italy	Europe
2016	China Gezhouba Group Corporation	Lao government	70.00	Newly-established	Production and supply of power, gas and water	Production and supply of power, gas and water	Laos	Asia
2016	CMC Holdings	NextVR Inc.	20.00	Merger and acquisition	Culture, sport and entertainment	Information transmission, computer service and software	USA	North America
2016	Zhejiang Kaishan Compressor Co., Ltd.	Xped Limited and PTBP		Merger and acquisition	Manufacturing	Production and supply of power, gas and water	Indonesia	Asia
2016	De Feng Lida Group	Mr. DjiminEdi		Merger and acquisition	Comprehensive	Real estate	Indonesia	Asia
2016	WuXi AppTec Group			Newly-established	Manufacturing	Manufacturing	USA	North America
2016	Hunan Dakang International Food & Agriculture Co., Ltd.	Land Information New Zealand		Merger and acquisition	Agriculture, forestry, animal husbandry and fishing	Agriculture, forestry, animal husbandry and fishing	New Zealand	Oceania
2016	China Capital Investment Group		19.00	Merger and acquisition	Financial	Real estate	Australia	Oceania

(continued)

(continued)

Year	Investor	Counterparty	Transaction amount (million dollars)	Investment method	Industry of investor (first level)	Industry of target	Country/Region of target	Continent
2016	Focuslight Technologies Inc.	Leimeng Optoeletronics (Hong Kong) Co., Ltd.	32.46	Merger and acquisition	Manufacturing	Manufacturing	Germany	Europe
2016	Shandong Qihe Biotechnology Co., Ltd.		4.46	Newly-established	Manufacturing	Manufacturing	Japan	Asia
2016	Alibaba Group	Thrive Global		Merger and acquisition	Information transmission, computer service and software	Culture, sport and entertainment	USA	North America
2016	Shanghai Electric Group Company Limited	TEC4AERO GmbH	188.60	Merger and acquisition	Manufacturing	Manufacturing	Germany	Europe
2016	Baidu, Inc.	Velodyne LiDAR	75.00	Merger and acquisition	Information transmission, computer service and software	Manufacturing	USA	North America
2016	Alibaba Group	Paytm		Merger and acquisition	Information transmission, computer service and software	Information transmission, computer service and software	India	Asia
2016	Jingrui Holdings Limited	Property Sky Limited	117.36	Merger and acquisition	Real estate	Resident service and other service	UK	North America
2016	Enjoyor Co., Ltd.	Magic Leap	5.00	Merger and acquisition	Information transmission, computer service and software	Information transmission, computer service and software	USA	North America
2016	Shanghai Electric Group Company Limited	Broetje Automation	197.96	Merger and acquisition	Manufacturing	Manufacturing	Germany	Europe

(continued)

(continued)

Year	Investor	Counterparty	Transaction amount (million dollars)	Investment method	Industry of investor (first level)	Industry of target	Country/Region of target	Continent
2016	Shandong Tyan Home Co., Ltd.	Conquest Mining	39.90	Merger and acquisition	Real estate	Mining	Australia	Oceania
2016	China Communications Construction Company	IDE Technologies		Merger and acquisition	Construction	Irrigation, environment and infrastructure management	Israel	Asia
2016	Tencent Technology (shenzhen) Company Limited	Hike Messenger		Merger and acquisition	Information transmission, computer service and software	Information transmission, computer service and software	India	Asia
2016	Transfar Zhilian Co., Ltd.	TPC Holding B.V	123	Merger and acquisition	Manufacturing	Manufacturing	Holland	Europe
2016	Greenland Holding Group Company Limited			Merger and acquisition	Real estate	Real estate	USA	North America
2016	Ping An Trust Co., Ltd.			Merger and acquisition	Financial	Real estate	USA	North America
2016	Agile Property Holdings Ltd.			Merger and acquisition	Real estate	Real estate	USA	North America
2016	Alibaba Group	Shopclues		Merger and acquisition	Information transmission, computer service and software	Information transmission, computer service and software	India	Asia
2016	Lonsen, Inc.	Emerald Performance Materials, LLC	130.40	Merger and acquisition	Manufacturing	Manufacturing	USA	North America
2016	CRRC Corporation Limited	印度先锋贸易公司		Newly-established	Manufacturing	Manufacturing	India	Asia
2016	China Wuyi Co., Ltd.		101	Newly-established	Construction	Construction	Kenya	Africa

(continued)

(continued)

Year	Investor	Counterparty	Transaction amount (million dollars)	Investment method	Industry of investor (first level)	Industry of target	Country/Region of target	Continent
2016	HNA Group (International) Company Limited	Great Eagle Holdings Limited	255	Merger and acquisition	Comprehensive	Real estate	USA	North America
2016	Cathay Capital Private Equity	Alkemics		Merger and acquisition	Financial	Information transmission, computer service and software	France	Europe
2016	Beijing ShuZhi Technology Co., Ltd.	Starbuster TMT Investments	900	Merger and acquisition	Information transmission, computer service and software	Information transmission, computer service and software	India	Asia
2016	Kunshan Kinglai Hygienic Materials Co., Ltd.	GNB Corporation	3.9	Merger and acquisition	Manufacturing	Manufacturing	USA	North America
2016	China Yangtze Power Co., Ltd.	BCP Meerwind Cayman Limited	215.16	Merger and acquisition	Production and supply of power, gas and water	Production and supply of power, gas and water	Germany	Europe
2016	China Three Gorges Corporation	BCP Meerwind Cayman Limited	501.91	Merger and acquisition	Production and supply of power, gas and water	Production and supply of power, gas and water	Germany	Europe
2016	Yango Group Co., Ltd.	Phoenix Holdings Ltd.	501.7043	Merger and acquisition	Comprehensive	Financial	Israel	Asia
2016	HuaPont Life Sciences Co.. Ltd.	Histogen, Inc.	6	Merger and acquisition	Manufacturing	Manufacturing	USA	North America
2016	COFCO Corporation	Cygne BV		Merger and acquisition	Manufacturing	Manufacturing	Holland	Europe
2016	Apex Microelectronics Co., Ltd.	Lexmark International, Inc. 1	2700	Merger and acquisition	Manufacturing	Manufacturing	USA	North America

(continued)

(continued)

Year	Investor	Counterparty	Transaction amount (million dollars)	Investment method	Industry of investor (first level)	Industry of target	Country/Region of target	Continent
2016	Beijing Xinwei Technology Group, Co., Ltd.	Space-Communication Ltd.	285	Merger and acquisition	Information transmission, computer service and software	Information transmission, computer service and software	Israel	Asia
2016	Ausnutria Dairy Corporation Ltd.	Nutrition Care	23.51	Merger and acquisition	Manufacturing	Manufacturing	Australia	Oceania
2016	Guangxi Normal University Press	Antique Collectors Club		Merger and acquisition	Culture, sport and entertainment	Culture, sport and entertainment	UK	Europe
2016	GCL-Poly Energy Holdings Limited	SunEdison	150	Merger and acquisition	Production and supply of power, gas and water	Production and supply of power, gas and water	USA	North America
2016	Chervon Holdings Ltd.	Robert Bosch GmbH		Merger and acquisition	Manufacturing	Manufacturing	USA	North America
2016	Vanfund Urban Investment & Development Co., Ltd.	Osterhout Group, Inc	14.61	Merger and acquisition	Real estate	Manufacturing	USA	North America
2016	Huayi Brothers International Limited	Russo Brothers	250	Newly-established	Culture, sport and entertainment	Culture, sport and entertainment	USA	North America
2016	China Zhongwang Holdings Limited	Aleris Corporation	2330	Merger and acquisition	Manufacturing	Manufacturing	USA	North America
2016	Chiho-Tiande Group Limited	Scholz Holding GMBH		Merger and acquisition	Manufacturing	Manufacturing	Germany	Europe
2016	Shanghai Raas Blood Products Co., Ltd.	Bio Products Laboratory Ltd.	1153.7805	Merger and acquisition	Manufacturing	Manufacturing	UK	Europe
2016	Shanghai Cooltech Power Co., Ltd.	Modell Enterprises Ltd. and Mr Trevor Modell	9.10	Merger and acquisition	Manufacturing	Manufacturing	UK	Europe

(continued)

(continued)

Year	Investor	Counterparty	Transaction amount (million dollars)	Investment method	Industry of investor (first level)	Industry of target	Country/Region of target	Continent
2016	China National Chemical Corporation	Discount Investment Corporation Ltd.	1400	Merger and acquisition	Manufacturing	Manufacturing	Israel	Asia
2016	Shanghai Electric Group Company Limited	K-Electric Ltd.	1600	Merger and acquisition	Manufacturing	Manufacturing	Pakistan	Asia
2016	Tencent Technology (shenzhen) Company Limited	FreeCharge	150	Merger and acquisition	Information transmission, computer service and software	Information transmission, computer service and software	India	Asia
2016	SRE Group		109.86	Merger and acquisition	Financial	Real estate	UK	Europe
2016	VGRASS Fashion Co., Ltd.	E-Land Group	840.89	Merger and acquisition	Manufacturing	Manufacturing	Korea	Asia
2016	Ant Financial Services Group	Tricon Global Restaurant, Inc.	50	Merger and acquisition	Financial	Lodging and catering	USA	North America
2016	Capital Environment Holdings Limited	BCG NZ Investment Holding Limited	234	Merger and acquisition	Irrigation, environment and infrastructure management	Irrigation, environment and infrastructure management	New Zealand	Oceania
2016	Zanyu Technology Group Co., Ltd.	PT.Dua Kuda Indonesia		Merger and acquisition	Manufacturing	Manufacturing	Indonesia	Asia
2016	China Vanke Co., Ltd.		148.994	Merger and acquisition	Real estate	Real estate	UK	Europe
2016	China International Marine Containers (Group) Co., Ltd.	Pteris Global Limited	55.47	Merger and acquisition	Manufacturing	Transportation, storage and post	Singapore	Asia
2016	Chongqing Tianci Hot Springs (Group) Co., Ltd.		31.95	Merger and acquisition	Lodging and catering	Lodging and catering	France	Europe

(continued)

(continued)

Year	Investor	Counterparty	Transaction amount (million dollars)	Investment method	Industry of investor (first level)	Industry of target	Country/Region of target	Continent
2016	Chongqing Tianci Hot Springs (Group) Co., Ltd.		18.25	Merger and acquisition	Lodging and catering	Manufacturing	France	Europe
2016	Fosun Group	NAGICO Holdings Limited		Merger and acquisition	Comprehensive	Financial	Caribbean	North America, South America
2016	Jilin Jien Nickel Industry Co., Ltd.	Quebec Lithium Inc.	75.68	Merger and acquisition	Mining	Mining	Canada	North America
2016	Tianqi Lithium Corporation	Pampa		Merger and acquisition	Manufacturing	Manufacturing	Chile	South America
2016	Vitop BIOenergy (China) Limited	ECrent Holdings Limited		Merger and acquisition	Manufacturing	Information transmission, computer service and software	USA	North America
2016	Ant Financial Services Group	EyeVerify	70	Merger and acquisition	Financial	Scientific research, technology service and geological survey	USA	North America
2016	Shanghai Zhongji Investment Holding Co., Ltd.	Macro Shots Network	240.76	Merger and acquisition	Information transmission, computer service and software	Information transmission, computer service and software	UK	Europe
2016	Kuang-Chi Technologies Co., Ltd.	Agent Video Intelligence	4.3	Merger and acquisition	Scientific research, technology service and geological survey	Scientific research, technology service and geological survey	Israel	Asia
2016	China Minsheng Investment Co., Ltd.		42.23	Merger and acquisition	Financial	Real estate	UK	Europe

(continued)

(continued)

Year	Investor	Counterparty	Transaction amount (million dollars)	Investment method	Industry of investor (first level)	Industry of target	Country/Region of target	Continent
2016	Gionee Communication Equipment Co., Ltd.		73.02	Newly-established	Manufacturing	Manufacturing	India	Asia
2016	Jinhe Biotechnology Co., Ltd.	ProtaTek International, Inc.	20	Merger and acquisition	Manufacturing	Manufacturing	USA	North America
2016	China Investment Corporation			Merger and acquisition	Financial	Transportation, storage and post	Australia	Oceania
2016	WoSign CA Limited	StartCom CA Limited		Merger and acquisition	Scientific research, technology service and geological survey	Scientific research, technology service and geological survey	Israel	Asia
2016	Qingdao Publishing Group	日本渡边淳一文学馆		Merger and acquisition	Culture, sport and entertainment	Culture, sport and entertainment	Japan	Asia
2016	Guangdong Guangken Rubber Group Co., Ltd.	Thai Hua Rubber Public Company Limited	265.51	Merger and acquisition	Manufacturing	Manufacturing	Thailand	Asia
2016	China Pacific Insurance (group) Co., Ltd.	Metromile	50	Merger and acquisition	Financial	Financial	USA	North America
2016	Wei Long Grape Wine Co., Ltd.		9.89	Merger and acquisition	Manufacturing	Manufacturing	Australia	Oceania
2016	北京山海昆仑资本管理有限公司	Analogix Semiconductor	500	Merger and acquisition	Financial	Manufacturing	USA	North America
2016	Panda Green Energy Group Limited	Notus Investments	39.52	Merger and acquisition	Production and supply of power, gas and water	Production and supply of power, gas and water	UK	Europe
2016	Jiangsu Lantian Aerospace Industry Park	Panstwowe Zaklady Lotnicze		Merger and acquisition	Manufacturing	Manufacturing	Poland	Europe

(continued)

(continued)

Year	Investor	Counterparty	Transaction amount (million dollars)	Investment method	Industry of investor (first level)	Industry of target	Country/Region of target	Continent
2016	China Tian Ying Inc.	Actividades de Construcciones y Servicios	8800	Merger and acquisition	Irrigation, environment and infrastructure management	Irrigation, environment and infrastructure management	Spain	Europe
2016	Orient Hontai Capital	Applovin	1400	Merger and acquisition	Financial	Information transmission, computer service and software	USA	North America
2016	Hangzhou Contact Information Technology Co., Ltd.	Newegg. Inc	264.17	Merger and acquisition	Information transmission, computer service and software	Information transmission, computer service and software	USA	North America
2016	Shenghe Resources Holding Co., Ltd.	Greenland Minerals Ltd.	3.48	Merger and acquisition	Mining	Mining	Denmark	Europe
2016	China COSCO Shipping Corporation Limited	Abu Dhabi Port Authority	738	Newly-established	Transportation, storage and post	Transportation, storage and post	UAE	Asia
2016	China General Nuclear Power Corporation	WindVision Belgium S.A.		Merger and acquisition	Production and supply of power, gas and water	Production and supply of power, gas and water	Belgium	Europe
2016	China Construction Bank	PT Bank Windu Kentjana International Tbk		Merger and acquisition	Financial	Financial	Indonesia	Asia
2016	Geo-Jade Petroleum Corparation	班克斯公司		Merger and acquisition	Manufacturing	Manufacturing	Canada	North America
2016	Shanghai Electric Group Company Limited	Fabbrica Italiana Automobili Torino,F.I.A.T.		Merger and acquisition	Manufacturing	Manufacturing	Italy	Europe
2016	China Molybdenum Co., Ltd.	Anglo American plc	1700	Merger and acquisition	Manufacturing	Manufacturing	Brazil	South America
2016	China Science & Merchants Capital Management Group	Founders Factory		Merger and acquisition	Financial	Information transmission, computer service and software	UK	Europe

(continued)

(continued)

Year	Investor	Counterparty	Transaction amount (million dollars)	Investment method	Industry of investor (first level)	Industry of target	Country/Region of target	Continent
2016	Qianhai Financial Holdings Co., Ltd.	ACR Capital Holdings Pte Ltd.	1000.00	Merger and acquisition	Financial	Financial	Singapore	Asia
2016	China Everbright Group	Tirana International Airport		Merger and acquisition	Financial	Resident service and other service	Albania	Europe
2016	China Three Gorges Corporation	Duke Energy	1200	Merger and acquisition	Production and supply of power, gas and water	Production and supply of power, gas and water	Brazil	South America
2016	Chengdu Techcent Environment Co., Ltd.	ALBA Group	324.51	Merger and acquisition	Irrigation, environment and infrastructure management	Irrigation, environment and infrastructure management	Germany	Europe
2016	Beijing Gaea Interactive Entertainment Co., Ltd.	KABAM INC	8.00	Merger and acquisition	Culture, sport and entertainment	Culture, sport and entertainment	USA	North America
2016	Guirenniao Co., Ltd.	AND1	26.00	Merger and acquisition	Manufacturing	Manufacturing	USA	North America
2016	Shanghai Yiguo E-Commerce Co., Ltd.	SunMoon Food	24.00	Merger and acquisition	Wholesale and retail	Agriculture, forestry, animal husbandry and fishing	USA	North America
2016	Alibaba Group	PlaceIQ	2.5	Merger and acquisition	Information transmission, computer service and software	Information transmission, computer service and software	USA	North America
2016	Shanghai Jin Jiang International Hotels (Group) Company Limited	WeWork Cos.	260.00	Merger and acquisition	Lodging and catering	Real estate	USA	North America

(continued)

(continued)

Year	Investor	Counterparty	Transaction amount (million dollars)	Investment method	Industry of investor (first level)	Industry of target	Country/Region of target	Continent
2016	Chongqing New Century Cruise Co., Ltd.	Playtika Holding Corp.		Merger and acquisition	Information transmission, computer service and software	Information transmission, computer service and software	USA	North America
2016	Chongqing Sokon Industry Group Stock Co., Ltd.	AC Propulsion Inc.	95.00	Merger and acquisition	Manufacturing	Manufacturing	USA	North America
2016	Beijing Byte Dance Telecommunications Co., Ltd.	Dailyhunt	25.00	Merger and acquisition	Information transmission, computer service and software	Information transmission, computer service and software	Indonesia	Asia
2016	Shangying Group	Oneworld Star International Holdings Limited	280	Merger and acquisition	manufacturing	manufacturing	USA	North America
2016	Ruyi Group	SMCP Group	1480.96	Merger and acquisition	Manufacturing	Manufacturing	France	Europe
2016	The Holding of GeekBang (Beijing) Co., Ltd.	InfoQ		Merger and acquisition	Information transmission, computer service and software	Information transmission, computer service and software	USA	North America
2016	CEC Capital Corporation	Siemer & Associates(S&A)		Merger and acquisition	Financial	Financial	USA	North America
2016	Bank of China (Hong Kong) Limited	Bank of China (Malaysia) Berhad		Merger and acquisition	Financial	Financial	Malaysia	Asia
2016	China Life Insurance (Group) Company	Starwood Capital Group	2000.00	Merger and acquisition	financial	lodging and catering	USA	North America

(continued)

(continued)

Year	Investor	Counterparty	Transaction amount (million dollars)	Investment method	Industry of investor (first level)	Industry of target	Country/Region of target	Continent
2016	Comba Telecom Systems Holdings Ltd.	Transglory International Freight Co., Ltd.	5.00	Merger and acquisition	Information transmission, computer service and software	Information transmission, computer service and software	Laos	Asia
2016	China COSCO Holdings Co., Ltd.	APM Terminals	60.37	Merger and acquisition	Transportation, storage and post	Transportation, storage and post	Italy	Europe
2016	O.R.G Co., Ltd.	AJ Auxerre	7.97	Merger and acquisition	Manufacturing	Culture, sport and entertainment	France	Europe
2016	Beingmate Baby & Child Food Co., Ltd.	Fonterra Co-operative Group	63.35	Merger and acquisition	Manufacturing	Manufacturing	Australia	Oceania
2016	Modern Dental Group Limited	RTFP Dental Inc.	65	Merger and acquisition	Health, social security and social welfare	Health, social security and social welfare	USA	North America
2016	HC SemiTek Corporation	NSL, 和谐芯光	243.38	Merger and acquisition	Manufacturing	Manufacturing	USA	North America
2016	Yunnan Water Investment Limited	Galaxy New Spring Pte. Ltd.	136.5	Merger and acquisition	Irrigation, environment and infrastructure management	Irrigation, environment and infrastructure management	Singapore	Asia
2016	BYD Company Ltd.		22.3	Newly-established	Manufacturing	Manufacturing	Hungary	Europe
2016	China Investment Corporation	Government of the state of Victoria, Australia		Merger and acquisition	Financial	Transportation, storage and post	Australia	Oceania
2016	Ant Financial Services Group	Ascend Money		Merger and acquisition	Financial	Information transmission, computer service and software	Thailand	Asia
2016	HNA Group (International) Company Limited	UAS International Trip Support		Merger and acquisition	Comprehensive	Leasing and business service industry	USA	North America

(continued)

(continued)

Year	Investor	Counterparty	Transaction amount (million dollars)	Investment method	Industry of investor (first level)	Industry of target	Country/Region of target	Continent
2016	Shanghai Electric Power Co., Ltd.	Abraaj Group	1770	Merger and acquisition	Production and supply of power, gas and water	Production and supply of power, gas and water	Pakistan	Asia
2016	Xiwang Iovate Holdings Company Limited	Kerr Investment Holdings Corp.	503.44	Merger and acquisition	Manufacturing	Manufacturing	USA	North America
2016	Weichai Power Co., Ltd.	DH Services Luxembourg Holding S.à.r.l	2100	Merger and acquisition	Manufacturing	Transportation, storage and post	Germany	Europe
2016	Evergrande Group	Cala Homes	857	Merger and acquisition	Real estate	Real estate	UK	Europe
2016	Aluminum Corporation of China	Rio Tinto Australia		Merger and acquisition	Manufacturing	Mining	Guinea	Africa
2016	Solomon Systech Limited	Microchip Technology Incorporated	23	Merger and acquisition	Manufacturing	Manufacturing	USA	North America
2016	China Oceanwide Holdings Group	Quam Capital Limited	140	Merger and acquisition	Comprehensive	Financial	Hong Kong	Asia
2016	HNA Technology Co., Ltd.	Ingram Micro Inc.(IMI)	6009	Merger and acquisition	Transportation, storage and post	Information transmission, computer service and software	USA	North America
2016	Beijing Kunlun Tech Co., Ltd.	Opera Software AS	200	Merger and acquisition	Information transmission, computer service and software	Information transmission, computer service and software	Norway	Europe
2016	Beijing Qihu Keji Co., Ltd.	Opera Software AS		Merger and acquisition	Information transmission, computer service and software	Information transmission, computer service and software	Norway	Europe

(continued)

(continued)

Year	Investor	Counterparty	Transaction amount (million dollars)	Investment method	Industry of investor (first level)	Industry of target	Country/Region of target	Continent
2016	Golden Brick Capital Private Equity Fund I L.P	Opera Software AS		Merger and acquisition	Financial	Information transmission, computer service and software	Norway	Europe
2016	China CITIC Bank	Halyk Bank		Merger and acquisition	Financial	Financial	Kazakhstan	Asia
2016	Han's Laser Technology Industry Group Co., Ltd.	Coractive High-Tech Inc.	25.2	Merger and acquisition	Manufacturing	Manufacturing	Canada	North America
2016	Cubespace Corporation Limited	Friant Associates	78	Merger and acquisition	Manufacturing	Manufacturing	USA	North America
2016	Leyard Optoelectronic Co., Ltd.	NaturalPoint, Inc.	125	Merger and acquisition	Scientific research, technology service and geological survey	Scientific research, technology service and geological survey	USA	North America
2016	Chuang's China Investments Limited	Standard Life	99.75	Merger and acquisition	Real estate	Real estate	UK	Europe
2016	Jiangsu Zhongnan Construction Group Co., Ltd.	PeerNova, Inc	4	Merger and acquisition	Construction	Scientific research, technology service and geological survey	USA	North America
2016	SEA Group	PFM EuroSelect Elf GmbH & Co KG, Lapis Grundstücksverwaltungs-GmbH	190.94	Merger and acquisition	Real estate	Real estate	UK	Europe
2016	Beijing Enterprises Holdings Limited	Rosneft Oil Company	1100	Merger and acquisition	Production and supply of power, gas and water	Mining	Russia	Europe
2016	Shandong Shipping Co., Ltd.	DSD Shipping AS		Merger and acquisition	Transportation, storage and post	Transportation, storage and post	Norway	Europe

(continued)

(continued)

Year	Investor	Counterparty	Transaction amount (million dollars)	Investment method	Industry of investor (first level)	Industry of target	Country/Region of target	Continent
2016	Hakim Unique internet Co., Ltd.	BIGFACE Corporation	0.0708	Merger and acquisition	Information transmission, computer service and software	Culture, sport and entertainment	Japan	Asia
2016	Haitong Securities Company Limited	Haitong Securities India Private Limited	13.77	Merger and acquisition	Financial	Financial	India	Asia
2016	Hytera Communications Co., Ltd.	Sepura Limited	100	Merger and acquisition	Manufacturing	Manufacturing	UK	Europe
2016	Southwest Energy & Mineral Inc.	MAS Holdings Pvt. Ltd.		Merger and acquisition	Mining	Mining	Australia	Oceania
2016	China Animation Characters Company Limited	Sega Live Creation Inc. (SLC)		Merger and acquisition	Culture, sport and entertainment	Culture, sport and entertainment	Japan	Asia
2016	China Baoli Technologies Holdings Limited	Telconet Capital		Merger and acquisition	Financial	Financial	Russia	Europe
2016	Alibaba Group	Tokyo Broadcasting System, Inc.		Merger and acquisition	Information transmission, computer service and software	Culture, sport and entertainment	Japan	Asia
2016	Zhejiang Crystal-Optech Co., Ltd.	Lumus Optical	10.2	Merger and acquisition	Manufacturing	Scientific research, technology service and geological survey	Israel	Asia
2016	Comtec Solar Systems Group Limited	富林(亚洲)	7.61	Merger and acquisition	Manufacturing	Production and supply of power, gas and water		
2016	Shaanxi J&R Optimum Energy Co., Ltd.	Altura Mining Limited	31.43	Merger and acquisition	Manufacturing	Mining	Australia	Oceania
2016	Wanda Group	Odeon & UCI		Merger and acquisition	Comprehensive	Culture, sport and entertainment	USA	North America

(continued)

(continued)

Year	Investor	Counterparty	Transaction amount (million dollars)	Investment method	Industry of investor (first level)	Industry of target	Country/Region of target	Continent
2016	China Ocean Shipping(Group) Company	Subordinate Company of China Ocean Shipping(Group) Company	10.6	Merger and acquisition	Transportation, storage and post	Transportation, storage and post	Greece	Europe
2016	Shaanxi Ligeance Mineral Resources Co., Ltd.	Gardner Aerospace Holdings Limited	413	Merger and acquisition	Manufacturing	Manufacturing	UK	Europe
2016	GigaDevice Semiconductor (Beijing), Inc.	Integrated Silicon Solution		Merger and acquisition	Manufacturing	Manufacturing	USA	North America
2016	Fosun Group	Millennium bcp	184.72	Merger and acquisition	Comprehensive	Financial	Portugal	Europe
2016	WH Group Limited	Clougherty Packaging LLC	145	Merger and acquisition	Manufacturing	Manufacturing	USA	North America
2016	Wintime Energy Co., Ltd.	Hinkley Point Nuclear Power Project	439.17	Newly-established	Mining	Production and supply of power, gas and water	UK	Europe
2016	Shanghai Ctrip International Travel Services Co., Ltd.	Skyscanner Ltd.	17.4	Merger and acquisition	Information transmission, computer service and software	Resident service and other service	UK	Europe
2016	Guangdong Golden Glass Technologies Limited	前海喜诺, 纳兰德基金	355.07	Merger and acquisition	Manufacturing	Information transmission, computer service and software	Singapore	Asia
2016	北京中长石基信息技术股份有限公司	SnapShot	20.05	Merger and acquisition	Information transmission, computer service and software	Information transmission, computer service and software	Germany	Europe
2016	Tai United Holdings Limited	Brockton Capital FundIII L.P	57.14	Merger and acquisition	Comprehensive	Financial	UK	Europe

(continued)

(continued)

Year	Investor	Counterparty	Transaction amount (million dollars)	Investment method	Industry of investor (first level)	Industry of target	Country/Region of target	Continent
2016	Southern China Gold Environment Co., Ltd.	Ruhrpumpen, Inc.		Merger and acquisition	Manufacturing	Manufacturing	USA	North America
2016	LANCY Group Co., Ltd.	L&P Cosmetic Co., Ltd.	25.24	Merger and acquisition	Manufacturing	Manufacturing	Korea	Asia
2016	Yanzhou Coal Mining Company Limited	Rio Tinto Group	2450	Merger and acquisition	Mining	Manufacturing	Australia	Oceania
2016	Tianjin Bohai Commodity Exchange Co., Ltd.	乌克兰复兴开发银行	3	Merger and acquisition	Leasing and business service industry	Financial	Ukraine	Europe
2016	Suzhou Greenleaf Daily Commodity Co., Ltd.	Pulse Health Solutions	688	Merger and acquisition	Health, social security and social welfare	Health, social security and social welfare	Australia	Oceania
2016	Meinian Onehealth Healthcare (Group) Co., Ltd.	Siemens Healthineers	7.52	Newly-established	Health, social security and social welfare	Health, social security and social welfare	Germany	Europe
2016	Vanfund Urban Investment & Development Co., Ltd.	Osterhout Design Group	15	Merger and acquisition	Real estate	Scientific research, technology service and geological survey	USA	North America
2016	Alibaba Pictures Group Limited	Showtime Analytics		Merger and acquisition	Culture, sport and entertainment	Culture, sport and entertainment	Ireland	Europe
2016	KPC Pharmaceuticals, Inc.	RiMO Therapeutics, Inc.	3	Merger and acquisition	Manufacturing	Health, social security and social welfare	USA	North America
2016	Zhongxing Telecommunication Equipment Corporation	OEP	101.28	Merger and acquisition	Manufacturing	Manufacturing	Turkey	Europe
2016	Zhongfu Construction Co., Ltd.	The Plough at Cadsden		Merger and acquisition	Construction	Lodging and catering	UK	Europe

(continued)

(continued)

Year	Investor	Counterparty	Transaction amount (million dollars)	Investment method	Industry of investor (first level)	Industry of target	Country/Region of target	Continent
2016	China Financial Futures Exchange	Pakistan Stock Exchange Limited	总 85	Merger and acquisition	Financial	Financial	Pakistan	Asia
2016	Shanghai Stock Exchange	Pakistan Stock Exchange Limited	总 85	Merger and acquisition	Financial	Financial	Pakistan	Asia
2016	Shenzhen Stock Exchange	Pakistan Stock Exchange Limited	总 85	Merger and acquisition	Financial	Financial	Pakistan	Asia
2016	Zhejiang Huahai Pharmaceutical Co., Ltd.	Par Pharmaceutical, Inc.	14	Merger and acquisition	Manufacturing	Manufacturing	USA	North America
2016	China General Nuclear Power Group	Gaelectric		Merger and acquisition	Production and supply of power, gas and water	Production and supply of power, gas and water	Ireland	Europe
2016	Shanghai Cred Real Estate Stock Co., Ltd.	S. Kidman & Co., Ltd.	288	Merger and acquisition	Real estate	Agriculture, forestry, animal husbandry and fishing	Australia	Oceania
2016	Weichai Holding Group Co., Ltd.		189.84	Merger and acquisition	Manufacturing	Manufacturing	Germany	Europe
2016	HNA Group (International) Company Limited	CIT and its subsidiary CIT Leasing	10057	Merger and acquisition	Comprehensive	Transportation, storage and post	USA	North America
2016	Wanfeng Group Co., Ltd.	MLTH Holding Inc.	144.79	Merger and acquisition	Manufacturing	Manufacturing	Canada	North America
2016	Lenovo Group Limited	Fujitsu Global		Merger and acquisition	Manufacturing	Manufacturing	Japan	Asia
2016	Silk Road Fund Co., Ltd.	SIBUR International GmbH		Merger and acquisition	Financial	Manufacturing	Russia	Europe
2016	Shanda Group	Legg Mason		Merger and acquisition	Comprehensive	Leasing and business service industry	USA	North America

(continued)

(continued)

Year	Investor	Counterparty	Transaction amount (million dollars)	Investment method	Industry of investor (first level)	Industry of target	Country/Region of target	Continent
2016	Thunder Software Technology Co., Ltd.	Rightware	69.48	Merger and acquisition	Information transmission, computer service and software	Information transmission, computer service and software	Finland	Europe
2016	Aland (Jiangsu) Nutraceutical Co., Ltd.	Brunel Healthcare Manufacturing Limited & Biocare Limited		Merger and acquisition	Manufacturing	Manufacturing	UK	Europe
2016	Huawei Technologies Co., Ltd.	HexaTier and Toga Networks		Merger and acquisition	Manufacturing	Information transmission, computer service and software	Israel	Asia
2016	Spearhead IMC Group	Smaato Holding AG	148	Merger and acquisition	Culture, sport and entertainment	Culture, sport and entertainment	USA	North America
2016	Tencent Technology (shenzhen) Company Limited	Sanook		Merger and acquisition	Information transmission, computer service and software	Information transmission, computer service and software	Thailand	Asia
2016	Ruyi Group	YGM Trading Ltd.	117	Merger and acquisition	Manufacturing	Manufacturing	UK	Europe
2016	Aviation Industry Corporation of China, Ltd.	Thompson Aero Seating		Merger and acquisition	Manufacturing	Manufacturing	UK	Europe
2016	HNA Group (International) Company Limited	Rezidor Hotel Group		Merger and acquisition	Comprehensive	Lodging and catering	Sweden	Europe
2016	Gansu Gangtai Holding (Group) Co., Ltd.	悦隆实业	210.95	Merger and acquisition	Manufacturing	Manufacturing	Italy	Europe

(continued)

(continued)

Year	Investor	Counterparty	Transaction amount (million dollars)	Investment method	Industry of investor (first level)	Industry of target	Country/Region of target	Continent
2016	NavInfo Co., Ltd.	HERE Technologies		Merger and acquisition	Information transmission, computer service and software	Information transmission, computer service and software	Holland	Europe
2016	China CEFC Eneb vir 7'u py Company Limited	AIDU, Fluege.de and other related portals		Merger and acquisition	Mining	Information transmission, computer service and software	Germany	Europe
2016	Shandong Hengyuan Petrochemical Company Limited	Malaysian-Based Shell Refining Company	66.3	Merger and acquisition	Manufacturing	Manufacturing	Malaysia	Asia
2017	Aier EYE Hospital Group	AW Healthcare Management	18	Merger and acquisition	Health, social security and social welfare	Health, social security and social welfare	USA	North America
2017	Jiangxi Huang Shang Huang Group Food Co., Ltd.	Streamland Honey Group Ltd.		Merger and acquisition	Manufacturing	Manufacturing	New Zealand	Oceania
2017	Huawei Technologies Co., Ltd.	HexaTier	42	Merger and acquisition	Manufacturing	Information transmission, computer service and software	Israel	Asia
2017	Beijing Capital Development Holding (Group) Co., Ltd.	Samsung Asset Management Co., Ltd.	258.87	Merger and acquisition	Real estate	Leasing and business service industry	UK	Europe
2017	Beijing Xingguang Film & TV Equipment Technologies Co., Ltd.	Click spring Design Inc	4.5	Merger and acquisition	Culture, sport and entertainment	Leasing and business service industry	USA	North America
2017	Tong Petrotech Inc.	Lincolnshire Management, Inc.	95	Merger and acquisition	Mining	Manufacturing	USA	North America
2017	Landing International Development Limited	Algona Pte. Ltd	420	Merger and acquisition	Comprehensive	Leasing and business service industry	South Korea	Asia

(continued)

(continued)

Year	Investor	Counterparty	Transaction amount (million dollars)	Investment method	Industry of investor (first level)	Industry of target	Country/Region of target	Continent
2017	Beijing Xiaoju Technology Co., Ltd.	99 Taxi Transportation Application		Merger and acquisition	Information transmission, computer service and software	Information transmission, computer service and software	Brazil	South America
2017	Cultural Investment Holdings	Framestore		Merger and acquisition	Culture, sport and entertainment	Culture, sport and entertainment	UK	Europe
2017	China Merchants Land Limited	佳临物业	64.97	Merger and acquisition	Real estate	Real estate	Hong Kong	Asia
2017	ISI-GF Equipment (Wuhan) Corp., Ltd.	ISI Italia Srl.	10.5	Merger and acquisition	Manufacturing	Scientific research, technology service and geological survey	Italy	Europe
2017	Shunwei Inc.	Mech Mocha	2	Merger and acquisition	Financial	Information transmission, computer service and software	India	Asia
2017	Shanghai Electric Group Company Limited	Centrais Eletricas Brasileiras		Merger and acquisition	Manufacturing	Manufacturing	Brazil	South America
2017	CITIC Limited	McDonald's (China) Co., Ltd.	2080	Merger and acquisition	Financial	Lodging and catering	Hong Kong	Asia
2017	Sanpower Group Co., Ltd.	Valeant Pharmaceuticals International	819	Merger and acquisition	Wholesale and retail	Manufacturing	Canada	North America
2017	Baotou Hongbote Technology Co., Ltd.	Rhodia Operations S.A.S		Merger and acquisition	Manufacturing	Manufacturing	France	Europe
2017	Fosun International Ltd.	PBM RESP Holdings, LLC		Merger and acquisition	Comprehensive	Manufacturing	Sweden	Europe
2017	Lenovo Group Limited	Kopin Corporation		Newly-established	Manufacturing	Scientific research, technology service and geological survey	USA	North America

(continued)

(continued)

Year	Investor	Counterparty	Transaction amount (million dollars)	Investment method	Industry of investor (first level)	Industry of target	Country/Region of target	Continent
2017	SAIC Motor Corporation Limited	General Motors Halol factory in India		Merger and acquisition	Manufacturing	Manufacturing	UK	Europe
2017	Bloomage BioTechnology Corporation Limited	Revitacare	26	Merger and acquisition	Manufacturing	Manufacturing	France	Europe
2017	Fosun International Ltd.	AST集团	150	Merger and acquisition	Comprehensive	Real estate	Russia	Europe
2017	The Export-Import Bank of China	Invitel Zrt.	237.6	Merger and acquisition	Financial	Information transmission, computer service and software	Hungary	Europe
2017	D&R Asset Management Group Co., Ltd.	Taiyo Asset Management Pte. Ltd.	5.4	Merger and acquisition	Financial	Financial	Singapore	Asia
2017	Shiji Information Technology	Review Rank S.A.	29.45	Merger and acquisition	Scientific research, technology service and geological survey	Scientific research, technology service and geological survey	USA	North America
2017	Bank of China (Hong Kong) Limited	Bank of China (Thailand) Limited		Merger and acquisition	Financial	Financial	Thailand	Asia
2017	Yonghui Superstores Co., Ltd.	Daymon Worldwide	165	Merger and acquisition	Wholesale and retail	Wholesale and retail	USA	North America
2017	Contemporary Amperex Technology Co., Ltd.	Valmet Automotive Oy		Merger and acquisition	Manufacturing	Manufacturing	Finland	Europe
2017	Leysen Jewellery Inc.	Joaillerie Leysen Freres SA	4.85	Merger and acquisition	Manufacturing	Manufacturing	Belgium	Europe
2017	Estun Automation Co., Ltd.	Trio Motion Technology Ltd.	19.66	Merger and acquisition	Manufacturing	Scientific research, technology service and geological survey	UK	Europe

(continued)

(continued)

Year	Investor	Counterparty	Transaction amount (million dollars)	Investment method	Industry of investor (first level)	Industry of target	Country/Region of target	Continent
2017	Hong Kong Meisheng Culture Company Ltd.	JAKKS Pacific, Inc.	736.33	Merger and acquisition	Culture, sports and entertainment	Manufacturing	USA	North America
2017	Beijing Jingyuntong Technology Co., Ltd.	NXP Semiconductors	2750	Merger and acquisition	Manufacturing	Manufacturing	Holland	Europe
2017	Sun Media Group	Grapevine Logic		Merger and acquisition	Culture, sports and entertainment	Culture, sports and entertainment	USA	North America
2017	Midea Group	Servotronix Motion Control		Merger and acquisition	Manufacturing	Scientific research, technology service and geological survey	Israel	Asia
2017	VCANBIO Cell & Gene Engineering Corp., Ltd.	上海傲源投资管理有限公司		Merger and acquisition	Manufacturing	Scientific research, technology service and geological survey	USA	North America
2017	CMC Capital Partners	Formula E Holdings Limited		Merger and acquisition	Culture, sports and entertainment	Culture, sport and entertainment	USA	North America
2017	Hytera Communications Co., Ltd.	Sepura Plc.	98.7	Merger and acquisition	Manufacturing	Manufacturing	UK	Europe
2017	Beijing ByteDance Technology Co., Ltd.	Flipagram		Merger and acquisition	Information transmission, computer service and software	Information transmission, computer service and software	USA	North America
2017	China NetCenter Ltd.	CDN-Video	7.42	Merger and acquisition	Information transmission, computer service and software	Information transmission, computer service and software	Russia	Europe

(continued)

(continued)

Year	Investor	Counterparty	Transaction amount (million dollars)	Investment method	Industry of investor (first level)	Industry of target	Country/Region of target	Continent
2017	Tencent Holdings Ltd.	Go-Jek		Merger and acquisition	Information transmission, computer service and software	Information transmission, computer service and software	Indonesia	Asia
2017	Matrix Partners China	PerceptIn		Merger and acquisition	Financial	Scientific research, technology service and geological survey	USA	North America
2017	Shunwei Inc.	Truebil	3.00	Merger and acquisition	Financial	Information transmission, computer service and software	Indonesia	Asia
2017	Zhejiang Chimin Pharmaceutical Co., Ltd.	Linear Chemicals S.L	5.58	Merger and acquisition	Manufacturing	Manufacturing	Spain	Europe
2017	Zhongding Group Limited	Tristone Flowtech Holding S.A.S	196.00	Merger and acquisition	Manufacturing	Manufacturing	France	Europe
2017	Ant Financial Services Group	Kakao Pay	200.00	Merger and acquisition	Financial	Information transmission, computer service and software	South Korea	Asia
2017	Ant Financial Services Group	MYNT Holdings Ltd.		Merger and acquisition	Financial	Financial	Philippines	Asia
2017	Huayi Brothers Media Co., Ltd.	Lytro	60.00	Merger and acquisition	Culture, sport and entertainment	Scientific research, technology service and geological survey	USA	North America
2017	Recon Holding	Millennium Films		Merger and acquisition	Comprehensive	Culture, sports and entertainment	USA	North America
2017	Shandong Tyan Home Co., Ltd.	Hanking Australia Pty Ltd.		Merger and acquisition	Real estate	Mining	Australia	Oceania
2017	China National Petroleum Corporation	Abu Dhabi National Oil Company	1800.00	Merger and acquisition	Manufacturing	Manufacturing	UAE	Asia

(continued)

(continued)

Year	Investor	Counterparty	Transaction amount (million dollars)	Investment method	Industry of investor (first level)	Industry of target	Country/Region of target	Continent
2017	China NetCenter Ltd.	KDDI Corporation	184.77	Merger and acquisition	Information transmission, computer service and software	Information transmission, computer service and software	Japan	Asia
2017	Tencent Holdings Ltd.	Innovega Inc.		Merger and acquisition	Information transmission, computer service and software	Scientific research, technology service and geological survey	USA	North America
2017	China ZhenHuaOil Co., Ltd.	Chevron Corporation	2000.00	Merger and acquisition	Manufacturing	Manufacturing	Bangladesh	Asia
2017	Shanda Group	NIDA Rooms		Merger and acquisition	Comprehensive	Information transmission, computer service and software	Indonesia	Asia
2017	Anbang Insurance Group	Retirement Concepts Group	746.27	Merger and acquisition	Financial	Health, social security and social welfare	Canada	North America
2017	Ningbo David Medical Device Co., Ltd.	Babybloom Healthcare		Merger and acquisition	Manufacturing	Manufacturing	Holland	Europe
2017	COFCO Corporation	Nidera NV		Merger and acquisition	Manufacturing	Manufacturing	Holland	Europe
2017	Ruyi Group	YGM Trading Ltd.	117.00	Merger and acquisition	Manufacturing	Manufacturing	Hong Kong	Asia
2017	Alibaba Group	Paytm Ecommerce	177.00	Merger and acquisition	Information transmission, computer service and software	Information transmission, computer service and software	India	Asia

(continued)

(continued)

Year	Investor	Counterparty	Transaction amount (million dollars)	Investment method	Industry of investor (first level)	Industry of target	Country/Region of target	Continent
2017	Fosun International Ltd.	The Floow	16.57	Merger and acquisition	Comprehensive	Information transmission, computer service and software	UK	Europe
2017	Vision Group	Unicoba da Amazonia Ltda.	46.09	Merger and acquisition	Manufacturing	Manufacturing	Brazil	South America
2017	Jiangsu Yuyue Medical Equipment & Supply Co., Ltd.	Metrax GmbH		Merger and acquisition	Manufacturing	Manufacturing	Germany	Europe
2017	Alibaba Group Holding Limited	Reliance Group, SVB India Finance and SAP Ventures	900.00	Merger and acquisition	Information transmission, computer service and software	Information transmission, computer service and software	India	Asia
2017	Ningbo Baosi Energy Equipment Co., Ltd.	Access Precision Tools Pte Ltd.	10.65	Merger and acquisition	Manufacturing	Manufacturing	Singapore	Asia
2017	Alibaba Group Holding Limited	WayRay AG.		Merger and acquisition	Information transmission, computer service and software	Manufacturing	Switzerland	Europe
2017	China Investment Corporation	Airbnb, Inc.	100.00	Merger and acquisition	Financial	Lodging and catering	USA	North America
2017	Orient Victory Travel Group Company Limited	北园一波	0.93	Merger and acquisition	Financial	Lodging and catering	Japan	Asia
2017	China Fortune Land Development Co., Ltd.	Tin Nghia Corp.		Merger and acquisition	Real estate	Real estate	Vietnam	Asia
2017	Yunnan Water Investment Limited	Galaxy New Spring Pte. Ltd.	126.50	Merger and acquisition	Irrigation, environment and infrastructure management	Irrigation, environment and infrastructure	Singapore	Asia

(continued)

(continued)

Year	Investor	Counterparty	Transaction amount (million dollars)	Investment method	Industry of investor (first level)	Industry of target	Country/Region of target	Continent
2017	Huachangda Canada Holdings Inc	Solcz Group Inc.	18.10	Merger and acquisition	Manufacturing	Manufacturing	Canada	North America
2017	Shandong Kerui Petroleum Equipment Co., Ltd.	阿尔及利亚国家机械制造集团(AGM)下属子公司Poval		Newly-established	Manufacturing	Manufacturing	Algeria	Africa
2017	Tencent Holdings Ltd.	Flipkart Online Services Pvt Ltd.		Merger and acquisition	Information transmission, computer service and software	Information transmission, computer service and software	India	Asia
2017	HNA Group (International) Company Limited	Brookfield Property Partners LP and New York State Teachers Retirement System	2210.00	Merger and acquisition	Transportation, storage and post	Real estate	USA	North America
2017	Beijing Capital Development Holding (Group) Co., Ltd.	Grosvenor European Properties Limited	120.31	Merger and acquisition	Real estate	Real estate	UK	Europe
2017	Creditease Corp.	Trumid Financial LLC		Merger and acquisition	Financial	Financial	USA	North America
2017	Creditease Corp.	WeConvene Limited		Merger and acquisition	Financial	Financial	Finland	Europe
2017	Creditease Corp.	WorldCover		Merger and acquisition	Financial	Financial	USA	North America
2017	Fosun International Ltd.	PBM Capital Group		Merger and acquisition	Comprehensive	Manufacturing	Sweden	Europe
2017	Fosun International Ltd.	Le Travenues Technology Pvt. Ltd.	5.00	Merger and acquisition	Comprehensive	Information transmission, computer service and software	India	Asia
2017	Gobi Partners, Inc.	Jirnexu		Merger and acquisition	Financial	Financial	Malaysia	Asia

(continued)

(continued)

Year	Investor	Counterparty	Transaction amount (million dollars)	Investment method	Industry of investor (first level)	Industry of target	Country/Region of target	Continent
2017	Zhonghong Zhuoye Group Co., Ltd.	Blackstone Group LP	429.00	Merger and acquisition	Financial	Culture, sport and entertainment	USA	North America
2017	Rifa Holding Group	Airwork Holdings Ltd.	147.41	Merger and acquisition	Manufacturing	Transportation, storage and post	New Zealand	Oceania
2017	HNA Group (International) Company Limited	OM Asset Management PLC	446.00	Merger and acquisition	Transportation, storage and post	Financial	USA	North America
2017	Hytera Communications Co., Ltd.	Norsat International Incorporation	62.00	Merger and acquisition	Manufacturing	Manufacturing	Canada	North America
2017	Mls Co., Ltd.	OSRAM GmbH, OSRAM SYLVANIA INC.		Merger and acquisition	Manufacturing	Manufacturing	Germany	Europe
2017	Tencent Holdings Ltd.	Tesla Motors, Inc.	1778.00	Merger and acquisition	Information transmission, computer service and software	Manufacturing	USA	North America
2017	China Oceanwide Holdings Group	International Data Group	1000.00	Merger and acquisition	Comprehensive	Information transmission, computer service and software	USA	North America
2017	China CEFC Energy Company Limited	Cowen Group		Merger and acquisition	Comprehensive	Financial	USA	North America
2017	Bohai Harvest RST (Shanghai) Equity Investment Fund Management Co., Ltd.	Lundin	1136	Merger and acquisition	Financial	Mining	Congo	Africa
2017	HNA Innovation Finance Group	Glencore International AG	775.00	Merger and acquisition	Transportation, storage and post	Leasing and business service industry	Switzerland	Europe
2017	Fosun International Ltd.	The Naga Group AG	13.34	Merger and acquisition	Financial	Financial	Germany	Europe

(continued)

(continued)

Year	Investor	Counterparty	Transaction amount (million dollars)	Investment method	Industry of investor (first level)	Industry of target	Country/Region of target	Continent
2017	China Investment Corporation	Petroleo Brasileiro SA		Merger and acquisition	Financial	Transportation, storage and post	Brazil	South America
2017	Guangzhou R&F Properties Co., Ltd.	CLS Holding	197.22	Merger and acquisition	Real estate	Real estate	UK	Europe
2017	Shandong Gold Group Co., Ltd.	Barrick Gold Corporation	960.00	Merger and acquisition	Manufacturing	Manufacturing	Argentina	South America
2017	Great Wall Motor Company Limited	New Leon or San Louis Potosi, Mexico		Newly-established	Manufacturing	Manufacturing	Mexico	North America
2017	Creat Group Corporation	Biotest AG	1400.00	Merger and acquisition	Comprehensive	Manufacturing	Germany	Europe
2017	Unic Capital Management	Xcerra Corporation	580.00	Merger and acquisition	Financial	Manufacturing	USA	North America
2017	Ligeance Investments Limited	Gardner Aerospace Holdings Limited	409.52	Merger and acquisition	Manufacturing	Manufacturing	UK	Europe
2017	Zhejiang Zheneng Electric Power Co., Ltd.	Norte Energia S.A.		Merger and acquisition	Production and supply of power, gas and water	Production and supply of power, gas and water	Brazil	South America
2017	Aier EYE Hospital Group	Cl nica Baviera,S.A.	170	Merger and acquisition	Health, social security and social welfare	Health, social security and social welfare	Spain	Europe
2017	Haohai Healthcare Holdings (BVI) Co., Ltd.	Contamac Holdings Limited	31.2	Merger and acquisition	Manufacturing	Manufacturing	UK	Europe
2017	CMC Capital Group	Creative Artists Agency		Merger and acquisition	Culture, sport and entertainment	Culture, sport and entertainment	USA	North America

(continued)

(continued)

Year	Investor	Counterparty	Transaction amount (million dollars)	Investment method	Industry of investor (first level)	Industry of target	Country/Region of target	Continent
2017	Zplay (Beijing) Information Technology Co., Ltd.	Noodlecake Studios Inc.	4.24	Merger and acquisition	Information transmission, computer service and software	Information transmission, computer service and software	Canada	North America
2017	Ant Financial Services Group	HelloPay Group		Merger and acquisition	Financial	Financial	Singapore	Asia
2017	Tatwah Smartech Co., Ltd.	Topbest Coast Limited	73	Merger and acquisition	Manufacturing	Information transmission, computer service and software	Cyprus	Europe
2017	Agic Capital	The Gores Group	170	Merger and acquisition	Financial	Manufacturing	Germany	Europe
2017	HNA Group (International) Company Limited		1460	Merger and acquisition	Transportation, storage and post	Wholesale and retail	Switzerland	Europe
2017	HNA Group (International) Company Limited	奥德布雷希特建筑公司	8000	Merger and acquisition	Transportation, storage and post	Transportation, storage and post	Brazil	South America
2017	Zhengzhou Coal Mining Machinery Group Co., Ltd.	Bosch Group	610	Merger and acquisition	Manufacturing	Manufacturing	Germany	Europe
2017	C C Land Holdings Limited	British Land and Oxford Properties	1480	Merger and acquisition	Real estate	Real estate	UK	Europe
2017	HNA Group (International) Company Limited	Deutsche Bank		Merger and acquisition	Transportation, storage and post	Financial	Germany	Europe
2017	Truking Technology Limited	Romaco Pharmatechnik GmbH	168	Merger and acquisition	Manufacturing	Manufacturing	Germany	Europe

(continued)

(continued)

Year	Investor	Counterparty	Transaction amount (million dollars)	Investment method	Industry of investor (first level)	Industry of target	Country/Region of target	Continent
2017	Tencent Holdings Ltd.	GO-JEK Indonesia	1200	Merger and acquisition	Information transmission, computer service and software	Information transmission, computer service and software	Indonesia	Asia
2017	Creditease Corp.	Nav.com		Merger and acquisition	Financial	Information transmission, computer service and software	USA	North America
2017	Hangzhou Greatstar Industrial Co., Ltd.	Masco Corporation	125	Merger and acquisition	Manufacturing	Manufacturing	USA	North America
2017	Zhonghong Holding Co., Ltd.	衍昭公司	410	Merger and acquisition	Real estate	Leasing and business service industry	Luxembourg	Europe
2017	Inner Mongolia Yili Industrial Group Co., Ltd.	Danone Group	850	Merger and acquisition	Manufacturing	Manufacturing	USA	North America
2017	Tencent Holdings Ltd.	Pocket Gems Inc.	90	Merger and acquisition	Information transmission, computer service and software	Information transmission, computer service and software	USA	North America
2017	China Polymetallic Mining Limited	禾瑞山矿业	14.39	Merger and acquisition	Mining	Mining	Myanmar	Asia
2017	Camsing Global	POW! Entertainment	11.5	Merger and acquisition	Culture, sports and entertainment	Culture, sport and entertainment	USA	North America
2017	Safbon Water Service (Holding) Inc., Shanghai	Doosan Heavy Industries America Holdings Inc.	7.36	Merger and acquisition	Irrigation, environment and infrastructure management	Irrigation, environment and infrastructure	USA	North America

(continued)

(continued)

Year	Investor	Counterparty	Transaction amount (million dollars)	Investment method	Industry of investor (first level)	Industry of target	Country/Region of target	Continent
2017	Ctrip Travel Information Technology(Shanghai)Co., Ltd.	Etraveli		Merger and acquisition	Information transmission, computer service and software	Information transmission, computer service and software	Sweden	Europe
2017	Alibaba Group Holding Limited	Magic Leap		Merger and acquisition	Information transmission, computer service and software	Information transmission, computer service and software	USA	North America
2017	Healthoo International Technology Holdings Limited	Gene Sort Ltd.	13.96	Merger and acquisition	Financial	Health, social security and social welfare	Israel	Asia
2017	Aba Chemicals Corporation	AMINO CHEMICALS Limited	27.39	Merger and acquisition	Manufacturing	Manufacturing	Malta	Europe
2017	Shanghai Pharmaceuticals Holding Co., Ltd.	Stada Arzneimittel AG		Merger and acquisition	Manufacturing	Manufacturing	Germany	Europe
2017	Alibaba Group Holding Limited	Qupital Limited	2	Merger and acquisition	Information transmission, computer service and software	Financial	Hong Kong	Asia
2017	OCBC Bank (China) Co., Ltd.	National Australia Bank		Merger and acquisition	Financial	Financial	Australia	Oceania
2017	Beijing Union Pay Merchant Services Co., Ltd.	Merchant Support		Merger and acquisition	Financial	Financial	Japan	Asia
2017	Tianjin Motor Dies Co., Ltd.	DieTech	33	Merger and acquisition	Manufacturing	Manufacturing	USA	North America

(continued)

(continued)

Year	Investor	Counterparty	Transaction amount (million dollars)	Investment method	Industry of investor (first level)	Industry of target	Country/Region of target	Continent
2017	China Life Insurance (Group) Company	ElmTree Funds, LLC	950	Merger and acquisition	Financial	Real estate	USA	North America
2017	Everbright Securities Company Limited	North Square Blue Oak Ltd.		Merger and acquisition	Financial	Financial	UK	Europe
2017	Ausnutria Dairy Corporation Ltd.	Oz Farm Royal Pty Ltd.	8.8	Merger and acquisition	Manufacturing	Manufacturing	Australia	Oceania
2017	Ausnutria Dairy Corporation Ltd.	Australian Dairy Park Pty Ltd.	17.6	Merger and acquisition	Manufacturing	Manufacturing	Australia	Oceania
2017	China Resources (Holdings) Co., Ltd.		316	Merger and acquisition	Comprehensive	Real estate	UK	Europe
2017	Ningbo Jifeng Auto Parts Co., Ltd.	Grammer AG	67	Merger and acquisition	Manufacturing	Manufacturing	Germany	Europe
2017	Yanzhou Coal Mining Co., Ltd.	Mitsubishi Corporation (Australia)	700	Merger and acquisition	Mining	Mining	Australia	Oceania
2017	Fosun Group	Origin Energy	1500	Merger and acquisition	Comprehensive	Mining	Australia	Oceania
2017	CRRC Corporation Limited	Skoda Transportation	1279	Merger and acquisition	Manufacturing	Manufacturing	Czech Republic	Europe
2017	500彩票网	The Multi Group Ltd.	56	Merger and acquisition	Culture, sports and entertainment	Culture, sport and entertainment	Malta	Europe
2017	500彩票网	Melco International Development Limited	41.3	Merger and acquisition	Culture, sports and entertainment	Culture, sport and entertainment	Hong Kong	Asia
2017	Bright Dairy & Food Co., Ltd.	New Zealand Dairy Company	23.96	Merger and acquisition	Manufacturing	Manufacturing	New Zealand	Oceania
2017	Humanwell Healthcare (Group) Co., Ltd.	ANSELL Ltd.	360	Merger and acquisition	Manufacturing	Manufacturing	Australia	Oceania

(continued)

(continued)

Year	Investor	Counterparty	Transaction amount (million dollars)	Investment method	Industry of investor (first level)	Industry of target	Country/Region of target	Continent
2017	Shanghai Conant Macroflag Group Co., Ltd.	MCSabae Holdings Limited	10.73	Merger and acquisition	Manufacturing	Manufacturing	Hong Kong	Asia
2017	Suning.Com Co., Ltd.	京都出租车公司“爱媛交通”		Merger and acquisition	Manufacturing	Transportation, storage and post	Japan	Asia
2017	Jingrui Estate(Group) Co., Ltd.	Hong Leong Group	104.15	Merger and acquisition	Real estate	Real estate	Singapore	Asia
2017	Zhefu Holding Group Co., Ltd.	RD Group AS and ARD AS	7.69	Merger and acquisition	Manufacturing	Manufacturing	Norway	Europe
2017	ASR Microelectronics (Shanghai) Co., Ltd.	Marvell Technology Group Ltd.		Merger and acquisition	Information transmission, computer service and software	Information transmission, computer service and software	USA	North America
2017	Dalian Wanda Group Co., Ltd.	Competitor Group Holdings, Inc.		Merger and acquisition	Comprehensive	Culture, sport and entertainment	USA	North America
2017	Shandong Gold Mining Co., Ltd.	Barrick Gold Corporation	1260	Merger and acquisition	Mining	Mining	Argentina	South America
2017	Saic Motor Corporation Limited	General Motors Corporation		Merger and acquisition	Manufacturing	Manufacturing	India	Asia
2017	China Glass Holdings Limited			Merger and acquisition	Manufacturing	Manufacturing	Kazakhstan	Asia
2017	Alibaba Group Holding Limited	Orbgen Technologies Pvt. Ltd.		Merger and acquisition	Culture, sports and entertainment	Leasing and business service industry	India	Asia
2017	Yuan Cheng Cable Co., Ltd.	A&T Media, INC.	97.16	Merger and acquisition	Manufacturing	Culture, sport and entertainment	USA	North America
2017	China Galaxy Securities Co., Ltd.	CIMB Group Sdn Bhd	120	Merger and acquisition	Financial	Financial	Singapore	Asia

(continued)

(continued)

Year	Investor	Counterparty	Transaction amount (million dollars)	Investment method	Industry of investor (first level)	Industry of target	Country/Region of target	Continent
2017	China Citic Bank Corporation Limited	JSC Halyk Bank		Merger and acquisition	Financial	Financial	Kazakhstan	Asia
2017	Shanghai Shenda Co., Ltd.	International Automotive Components Group	310.8	Merger and acquisition	Manufacturing	Manufacturing	South Africa	Africa
2017	Shanghai Jahwa United Co., Ltd.	Arianna Global Limited	293	Merger and acquisition	Manufacturing	Manufacturing	Cayman Islands	North America
2017	Ganfeng Lithium Co., Ltd.	Lithium Americas Corp	49	Merger and acquisition	Manufacturing	Manufacturing	Canada	North America
2017	Beijing Bdstar Navigation Co., Ltd.	Friedrich & Wagner Holding GmbH	67.164	Merger and acquisition	Information transmission, computer service and software	Scientific research, technology service and geological survey	Germany	Europe
2017	Zhuzhou Times New Material Technology Co., Ltd.	Spencer Moulton	4.46	Merger and acquisition	Manufacturing	Manufacturing	France	Europe
2017	China Financial Services Holdings Limited	Thetford Grammar School		Merger and acquisition	Financial	Education	UK	Europe
2017	Yida International Investment Group Co., Ltd.	Esselunga S.p.A.	830	Merger and acquisition	Financial	Wholesale and retail	Italy	Europe
2017	State Power Investment Corporation	Latin American Power	370	Merger and acquisition	Production and supply of power, gas and water	Production and supply of power, gas and water	Chile	South America
2017	China Polymetallic Mining Limited	瑞丽纳迪有限公司	7.4	Merger and acquisition	Mining	Mining	Myanmar	Asia
2017	Fosun International Ltd.	Gemfields Plc	287	Merger and acquisition	Comprehensive	Mining	UK	Europe

(continued)

(continued)

Year	Investor	Counterparty	Transaction amount (million dollars)	Investment method	Industry of investor (first level)	Industry of target	Country/Region of target	Continent
2017	Zhonghong Zhuoye Group Co., Ltd.	Brookdale senior living	3000	Merger and acquisition	Comprehensive	Resident service and other service	USA	North America
2017	Tencent Holdings Ltd.	Rovio Entertainment Corporation	3000	Merger and acquisition	Information transmission, computer service and software	Information transmission, computer service and software	Finland	Europe
2017	Shenghe Resources Holding Co., Ltd.	Rare earth mine Mountain Pass	20.5	Merger and acquisition	Mining	Mining	USA	North America
2017	Boe Technology Group Co., Ltd.	SES-imagotag		Merger and acquisition	Manufacturing	Manufacturing	France	Europe
2017	Wus Printed Circuit (Kunshan) Co., Ltd.	Schweizer Electronic AG.		Merger and acquisition	Manufacturing	Manufacturing	Germany	Europe
2017	China Nonferrous Metal Industry Foreign Engineering And Construction Co., Ltd.	Gain & Win Pte. Ltd.	199	Merger and acquisition	Mining	Mining	Indonesia	Asia
2017	Hunan Dakang International Food & Agriculture Co., Ltd.	LandCo (Illinois Land Company)		Merger and acquisition	Agriculture, forestry, animal husbandry and fishing	Agriculture, forestry, animal husbandry and fishing	Brazil	South America
2017	Hunan Dakang International Food & Agriculture Co., Ltd.	Belagricola Comercioe Representaccoes de Produtos Agricolas S.A.		Merger and acquisition	Agriculture, forestry, animal husbandry and fishing	Agriculture, forestry, animal husbandry and fishing	Brazil	South America
2017	Ningbo Joyson Electronic Corp.	Preh IMA Automation GmbH	88.86	Merger and acquisition	Manufacturing	Manufacturing	France	Europe
2017	Vestate Group Holdings Limited	China Investment S.p.A.	37.85	Merger and acquisition	Leasing and business service industry	Real estate	Italy	Europe

(continued)

(continued)

Year	Investor	Counterparty	Transaction amount (million dollars)	Investment method	Industry of investor (first level)	Industry of target	Country/Region of target	Continent
2017	Zhejiang Xianju Pharmaceutical Co., Ltd.	Effechem S.r.l.	1.11	Merger and acquisition	Manufacturing	Manufacturing	Italy	Europe
2017	Zhejiang Xianju Pharmaceutical Co., Ltd.	Newchem S.P.A.	121.3	Merger and acquisition	Manufacturing	Manufacturing	Italy	Europe
2017	Yangtze River Industry Fund	RiteDose Holdings I, Inc.		Merger and acquisition	Financial	Manufacturing	USA	North America
2017	Robyn Hode Capital Limited	RiteDose Holdings I, Inc.		Merger and acquisition	Financial	Manufacturing	USA	North America
2017	Humanwell Healthcare (Group) Co., Ltd.	RiteDose Holdings I, Inc.		Merger and acquisition	Manufacturing	Manufacturing	USA	North America
2017	China Ocean Shipping(Group) Company	The Orient Overseas Container Line	4000	Merger and acquisition	Transportation, storage and post	Transportation, storage and post	Hong Kong	Asia
2017	Fosun International Ltd.			Merger and acquisition	Comprehensive	Real estate	Russia	Europe
2017	STATE GRID Corporation of China	Independent Power Transmission Operator	365.22	Merger and acquisition	Production and supply of power, gas and water	Production and supply of power, gas and water	Greece	Europe
2017	Qingdao Haier Co., Ltd.	Fisher & Paykel Production Machinery Limited	48.61	Merger and acquisition	Manufacturing	Manufacturing	New Zealand	Oceania
2017	Sichuan Yahua Industrial Group Co., Ltd.	Sequel Drill &Blast Pty Ltd.		Merger and acquisition	Manufacturing	Manufacturing	Australia	Oceania
2017	Beijing Jingdong Century Trading Co., Ltd.	Farfetch UK Limited	397.00	Merger and acquisition	Information transmission, computer service and software	Information transmission, computer service and software	UK	Europe
2017	Chongqing Sokon Industry Group Stock Co., Ltd.	AM General LLC	110.00	Merger and acquisition	Manufacturing	Manufacturing	USA	North America

(continued)

(continued)

Year	Investor	Counterparty	Transaction amount (million dollars)	Investment method	Industry of investor (first level)	Industry of target	Country/Region of target	Continent
2017	Geely Automobile Holdings Ltd.	PROTON Holdings Berhad		Merger and acquisition	Manufacturing	Manufacturing	Malaysia	Asia
2017	Geely Automobile Holdings Ltd.	Lotus Group International Limited		Merger and acquisition	Manufacturing	Manufacturing	UK	Europe
2017	Geely Automobile Holdings Ltd.	Terrafugia, Inc.		Merger and acquisition	Manufacturing	Manufacturing	USA	North America
2017	Inner Mongolia Berun Holding Group Company Ltd.		48.24	Merger and acquisition	Real estate	Real estate	Australia	Oceania
2017	Tianjin Haowu Electromechanical Product&Automobile Trade Co., Ltd.	FEUER powertrain GmbH & Co.		Merger and acquisition	Wholesale and retail	Manufacturing	Germany	Europe
2017	5Usport Media Co., Ltd.	British League A team Northampton		Merger and acquisition	Culture, sports and entertainment	Culture, sport and entertainment	UK	Europe
2017	ZhongZe Culture Investment Ltd.	Blue-Zoo Animation	92	Merger and acquisition	Culture, sports and entertainment	Culture, sport and entertainment	UK	Europe
2017	Pengxin International Mining Co., Ltd.	Tianhong Asset Management Co., Ltd.	288	Merger and acquisition	Mining	Mining	South Africa	Africa
2017	Desports Corporation	Italian League A team Parma		Merger and acquisition	Culture, sports and entertainment	Culture, sport and entertainment	Italy	Europe
2017	Fosun International Ltd.	PJSC Polyus	887.00	Merger and acquisition	Comprehensive	Manufacturing	Russia	Europe

(continued)

(continued)

Year	Investor	Counterparty	Transaction amount (million dollars)	Investment method	Industry of investor (first level)	Industry of target	Country/Region of target	Continent
2017	Alibaba Group Holding Limited	Lazada Group	1000.00	Merger and acquisition	Information transmission, computer service and software	Information transmission, computer service and software	Indonesia	Asia
2017	China International Trust and Investment Corporation Group		2208.47	Newly-established	Financial	Construction	UK	Europe
2017	China Investment Corporation	The Blackstone Group L.P.	13790.00	Merger and acquisition	financial	Transportation, storage and post	UK	Europe
2017	Zhejiang Kaishan Compressor Co., Ltd.	Presco Energy, LLC	3.00	Merger and acquisition	Manufacturing	Manufacturing	USA	North America
2017	中信现代农业产业投资基金	Dow Chemical Company	1100.00	Merger and acquisition	Agriculture, forestry, animal husbandry and fishing	Agriculture, forestry, animal husbandry and fishing	Brazil	South America
2017	Fosun International Ltd., Beijing Sanyuan Foods Co., Ltd.	Brassica TopCo S.A., PPN Management SAS	730.00	Merger and acquisition	Financial manufacturing	Manufacturing	France	Europe
2017	China Eastern Airlines Corporation Limited	Air France-KML	440.00	Merger and acquisition	Transportation, storage and post	Transportation, storage and post	France	Europe
2017	China Investment Corporation	TPG RE Finance Trust Inc.	190.00	Merger and acquisition	Financial	Real estate	USA	North America
2017	Shandong Gold Mining Co., Ltd.	Barrick Gold		Merger and acquisition	Manufacturing	Manufacturing	Canada	North America
2017	Hengkang Medical Group Co., Ltd.	PRP Diagnostic Imaging Pty Ltd.	264.65	Merger and acquisition	Manufacturing	Manufacturing	Australia	Oceania
2017	Wintime Energy Co., Ltd.	HRC Fertility Clinics	209	Merger and acquisition	Mining	Manufacturing	USA	North America

(continued)

(continued)

Year	Investor	Counterparty	Transaction amount (million dollars)	Investment method	Industry of investor (first level)	Industry of target	Country/Region of target	Continent
2017	Tencent Holdings Ltd.	Go-Jek	150	Merger and acquisition	Information transmission, computer service and software	Information transmission, computer service and software	Indonesia	Asia
2017	Lianhe Chemical Technology Co., Ltd.	Project Quartz Bidco Limited	127.98	Merger and acquisition	Manufacturing	Manufacturing	UK	Europe
2017	Tencent Holdings Ltd.	Frontier Developments	145.10	Merger and acquisition	Information transmission, computer service and software	Information transmission, computer service and software	UK	Europe
2017	China National Petroleum Corporation	Petrochemical Commercial Company		Newly-established	Manufacturing	Manufacturing	Iran	Asia
2017	HNA Group (International) Company Limited	Odebrecht Transport Aeroportos S.A.	19.80	Merger and acquisition	Transportation, storage and post	Transportation, storage and post	Brazil	South America
2017	Beijing Xiaoju Technology Co., Ltd.	Grab		Merger and acquisition	Information transmission, computer service and software	Information transmission, computer service and software	Singapore	Asia
2017	China Electro-mechanical Equipment Qiqiha'er Company	Kaz Munay Gas	350.00	Merger and acquisition	Manufacturing	Manufacturing	Romania	Europe
2017	Country Garden Holdings Co., Ltd.		300.00	Newly-established	Real estate	Real estate	Australia	Oceania
2017	Lenovo Group Limited	Precision Capital Pte. Ltd.	1760.00	Merger and acquisition	Manufacturing	Financial	Luxembourg	Europe

(continued)

(continued)

Year	Investor	Counterparty	Transaction amount (million dollars)	Investment method	Industry of investor (first level)	Industry of target	Country/Region of target	Continent
2017	Bluefocus Intelligent Communications Group Co., Ltd.	We Are Very Social Limited	10.40	Merger and acquisition	Information transmission, computer service and software	Information transmission, computer service and software	UK	Europe
2017	Beijing Bdstar Navigation Co., Ltd.	Rx Networks Inc.		Merger and acquisition	Manufacturing	Manufacturing	Canada	North America
2017	Hubei Forbon Technology Co., Ltd.	PST Industries		Merger and acquisition	Manufacturing	Manufacturing	Holland	Europe
2017	Shenzhen Grandland Group Co., Ltd.	LIXIL Group Corporation	546.00	Merger and acquisition	Construction	Construction	Japan	Asia
2017	China Three Gorges Corporation	Odebrecht Transport Aeroportos S.A.	1390.00	Merger and acquisition	Irrigation, environment and infrastructure management	Irrigation, environment and infrastructure	Peru	South America
2017	Nanjing Iron and Steel United Co., Ltd.	Koller Beteiligungs GmbH		Merger and acquisition	Manufacturing	Manufacturing	Germany	Europe
2017	Beijing Jingdong Century Trading Co., Ltd.	Go-Jek	100.00	Merger and acquisition	Information transmission, computer service and software	Information transmission, computer service and software	Indonesia	Asia
2017	Alibaba Group Holding Limited	PT Tokopedia	1100	Merger and acquisition	Information transmission, computer service and software	Information transmission, computer service and software	Indonesia	Asia
2017	Lander Sports Development Co., Ltd.	Premier League Southampton Club	234.00	Merger and acquisition	Culture, sports and entertainment	Culture, sport and entertainment	UK	Europe

(continued)

(continued)

Year	Investor	Counterparty	Transaction amount (million dollars)	Investment method	Industry of investor (first level)	Industry of target	Country/Region of target	Continent
2017	Beijing Jingdong Century Trading Co., Ltd.	Central Group	500.00	Merger and acquisition	Information transmission, computer service and software	Information transmission, computer service and software	Thailand	Asia
2017	HNA Group (International) Company Limited	Frankfurt–Hahn Airport	17.43	Merger and acquisition	Comprehensive	Transportation, storage and post	France	Europe
2017	Comba Telecom Systems(China) Limited	Enterprise of Telecommunications Lao	5.00	Merger and acquisition	Information transmission, computer service and software	Information transmission, computer service and software	Laos	Asia
2017	Gansu Gangtai Holding(Group) Co., Ltd.	Buccellati	225.50	Merger and acquisition	Wholesale and retail	Wholesale and retail	Italy	Europe
2017	Get Nice Holdings Limited	St. Andrew Street London LLC	27.60	Merger and acquisition	Financial	Real estate	UK	Europe
2017	Haiken Group	PT Kirana Megatara, Archipelago Rubber Trading Pte. Ltd.	137.00	Merger and acquisition	Financial	Manufacturing	Indonesia/ Singapore	Asia
2017	HNA Group (International) Company Limited	Government of Singapore Investment Corp, Temasek Holdings Private Limited		Merger and acquisition	Transportation, storage and post	Transportation, storage and post	Switzerland	Europe
2017	Beijing Oriental Yuhong Waterproof Technology Co., Ltd.	CAPAROL Beteiligungs-GmbH	27.70	Merger and acquisition	Manufacturing	Manufacturing	Germany	Europe
2017	Shenzhen Hepalink Pharmaceutical Group Co., Ltd.	Kymab Group Limited		Merger and acquisition	Manufacturing	Manufacturing	UK	Europe

(continued)

(continued)

Year	Investor	Counterparty	Transaction amount (million dollars)	Investment method	Industry of investor (first level)	Industry of target	Country/Region of target	Continent
2017	Shenzhen Longsys Electronics Company Limited	Lexar		Merger and acquisition	Manufacturing	Manufacturing	USA	North America
2017	Luxshare Precision Industry Co., Ltd.	ZF Friedrichshafen AG	1200.00	Merger and acquisition	Manufacturing	Manufacturing	Germany	Europe
2017	Xiaomi Inc.	ShareChat (Mohalla Tech Pvt. Ltd.)	15.60	Merger and acquisition	Manufacturing	Information transmission, computer service and software	India	Asia
2017	Shandong Yanzhou Mining Group	Mitsubishi Development Pty Ltd	230.00	Merger and acquisition	Mining	Mining	Australia	Oceania
2017	HNA Group (International) Company Limited	CWT Limited	1000.00	Merger and acquisition	Transportation, storage and post	Transportation, storage and post	Singapore	Asia
2017	China Merchants Group Co., Limited	TCP Participacoes S.A.	150	Merger and acquisition	Financial	Transportation, storage and post	Brazil	South America
2017	China Investment Corporation, China Life Insurance (Group) Company	InterPark		Merger and acquisition	Financial	Transportation, storage and post	USA	North America
2017	Cindat Capital Management Limited	Qhotels (Almarose Limited)		Merger and acquisition	Financial	Real estate	UK	Europe
2017	Alpha Group	FunnyFlux Co., Ltd.	16.20	Merger and acquisition	Culture, sports and entertainment	Culture, sport and entertainment	South Korea	Asia
2017	3SBio Group, China International Trust and Investment Corporation Group	Therapure	290.00	Merger and acquisition	Manufacturing financial	Manufacturing	Canada	North America
2017	Yanzhou Coal Mining Company Limited	Rio Tinto Group		Merger and acquisition	Mining	Mining	Australia	Oceania

(continued)

(continued)

Year	Investor	Counterparty	Transaction amount (million dollars)	Investment method	Industry of investor (first level)	Industry of target	Country/Region of target	Continent
2017	Beijing Bdstar Navigation Co., Ltd.	Friedrich & Wagner Holding GmbH	67.16	Merger and acquisition	Information transmission, computer service and software	Scientific research, technology service and geological survey	Germany	Europe
2017	Jiangsu Olive Sensors High-Tech Co., Ltd.	Schürholz GmbH, Schürholz GmbH & Co. KG Stanztechnik and Schürholz Polska Sp z o.o.	6.93	Merger and acquisition	Manufacturing	Manufacturing	Germany	Europe
2017	Dalian Zeus Entertainment Co., Ltd.	DotC United Inc.	340.00	Merger and acquisition	Culture, sports and entertainment	Information transmission, computer service and software	UK	Europe
2017	China Zhongwang Holdings Limited	Aluminiumwerk Unna AG	230.00	Merger and acquisition	Manufacturing	Manufacturing	Germany	Europe
2017	Guangdong Dongfang Precision Science & Technology Co., Ltd.	Fosber S.p.A.	38.30	Merger and acquisition	Manufacturing	Manufacturing	Italy	Europe
2017	Beijing Capital Agribusiness Group, CITIC Agriculture Investment Ltd.	Cherry Valley Farm	234.00	Merger and acquisition	Agriculture, forestry, animal husbandry and fishing	Agriculture, forestry, animal husbandry and fishing	UK	Europe
2017	Shanghai Pharmatech Co., Ltd	ResearchPoint Global		Merger and acquisition	Manufacturing	Manufacturing	USA	North America
2017	Zhonghong Holding Co., Ltd.	Abercrombie & Kent Group of Companies S.A.	412.00	Merger and acquisition	Real estate	Culture, sport and entertainment	USA	North America
2017	Hony Capital	Magnolia S.p.A.		Merger and acquisition	Financial	Manufacturing	Italy	Europe
2017	Hong Kong International Construction Investment Management Group Co., Ltd.	Sapphire Corporation Ltd.	34.00	Merger and acquisition	Construction	Construction	Singapore	Asia

(continued)

(continued)

Year	Investor	Counterparty	Transaction amount (million dollars)	Investment method	Industry of investor (first level)	Industry of target	Country/Region of target	Continent
2017	Shanying International Holdings Co., Ltd.	Nordic Paper Holding AB	270.14	Merger and acquisition	Manufacturing	Manufacturing	Sweden	Europe
2017	China Investment Corporation	Equis Energy	3700.00	Merger and acquisition	Financial	Production and supply of power, gas and water	Singapore	Asia
2017	Zhejiang Geely Holding Group Co., Ltd.	Tarrant Capital IP, LLC and Sinar Mas Group	311.00	Merger and acquisition	Manufacturing	Financial	Denmark	Europe
2017	Chengdu Kanghong Pharmaceutical Group Co., Ltd.	IOPtima Ltd.	46.72	Merger and acquisition	Manufacturing	Manufacturing	Israel	Asia
2017	Fosun International Ltd.	Gland Pharma Limited	1019.00	Merger and acquisition	Comprehensive	Manufacturing	India	Asia
2017	Shenzhen Energy Corporation	RE Mojave Holdings LLC RE Cantua Holdings LLC, RE Arabian Holdings LLC	232.00	Merger and acquisition	Production and supply of power, gas and water	Production and supply of power, gas and water	USA	North America
2017	Tencent Holdings Ltd.	Ola (ANI Technologies Pvt. Ltd.)		Merger and acquisition	Information transmission, computer service and software	Information transmission, computer service and software	India	Asia
2017	CHN ENERGY Investment Group Co., Ltd.	Copelouzos Group	3520.00	Merger and acquisition	Production and supply of power, gas and water	Production and supply of power, gas and water	Greece	Europe
2017	Ningbo Joyson Electronic Corp.	Kongsberg Automotive Holding ASA		Merger and acquisition	Manufacturing	Manufacturing	Norway	Europe
2017	China Vanke Co., Ltd., HOPU Investments, Hillhouse Capital Group, SMG Capital, Bank of China	Global Logistic Properties Ltd.	11600.00	Merger and acquisition	Comprehensive	Transportation, storage and post	Singapore	Asia

(continued)

(continued)

Year	Investor	Counterparty	Transaction amount (million dollars)	Investment method	Industry of investor (first level)	Industry of target	Country/Region of target	Continent
2017	New Hope Group Co., Ltd.	Real Pet Food Company		Merger and acquisition	Agriculture, forestry, animal husbandry and fishing	Agriculture, forestry, animal husbandry and fishing	Australia	Oceania
2017	China Aerospace Science and Technology Corporation	Erae Automotive Systems Co., Ltd.		Merger and acquisition	Manufacturing	Manufacturing	South Korea	Asia
2017	Ruyi Group	INVISTA	2000.00	Merger and acquisition	Manufacturing	Manufacturing	USA	North America
2017	Xiecheng Tourism Network Technology(Shanghai)Co., Ltd.	Twizoo		Merger and acquisition	Information transmission, computer service and software	Information transmission, computer service and software	UK	Europe
2017	Alibaba Group Holding Limited	Visualead	30.00	Merger and acquisition	Information transmission, computer service and software	Information transmission, computer service and software	Israel	Asia
2017	Xiecheng Tourism Network Technology(Shanghai)Co., Ltd.	Trip.com (Gogobot)		Merger and acquisition	Information transmission, computer service and software	Information transmission, computer service and software	UK	Europe
2017	Ruyi Group	Bagir Group		Merger and acquisition	Manufacturing	Manufacturing	Israel	Asia
2017	Nanjing Hicin Pharmaceutical Co., Ltd.	Nerviano Medical Sciences Group S.r.l		Merger and acquisition	Manufacturing	Manufacturing	Italy	Europe
2017	Luxin Venture Capital Group Co., Ltd.	StoreDot Ltd.	5.00	Merger and acquisition	Financial	Manufacturing	Israel	Asia

(continued)

(continued)

Year	Investor	Counterparty	Transaction amount (million dollars)	Investment method	Industry of investor (first level)	Industry of target	Country/Region of target	Continent
2017	Xiamen Kingdomway Group Company	PSupps Holdings, LLC	7.50	Merger and acquisition	Manufacturing	Manufacturing	USA	North America
2017	Shanghai New Eyes Medical Inc.	Medical Technical Products Limited Partnership	2.50	Merger and acquisition	Manufacturing	Manufacturing	USA	North America
2017	Geely Automobile Holdings Ltd.	TERRAFUGIA		Merger and acquisition	Manufacturing	Manufacturing	USA	North America
2017	Xiaomi Inc.	Youmi Co., Ltd.		Merger and acquisition	Manufacturing	Manufacturing	South Korea	Asia
2017	Dr.Peng Telecom & Media Group Co., Ltd.	Urban Communications Inc.	11.00	Merger and acquisition	Information transmission, computer service and software	Information transmission, computer service and software	Canada	North America
2017	Sundiro Holding Co., Ltd.	Lirtix S.A.and Rondatel S.A.	82.30	Merger and acquisition	Comprehensive	Manufacturing	Uruguay	South America
2017	Hengxin Shambala Culture Co., Ltd.	Pioneer Capital Pukeko LP Limited		Merger and acquisition	Culture, sports and entertainment	Culture, sport and entertainment	New Zealand	Oceania
2017	Saimo Electric Co., Ltd.	Epistolio S.r.l.	4.05	Merger and acquisition	Manufacturing	Manufacturing	Italy	Europe
2017	CEFC China Energy Company Limited	Central European Media Enterprises Ltd.		Merger and acquisition	Manufacturing	Culture, sport and entertainment	Czech Republic	Europe
2017	CEFC China Energy Company Limited	Montepio Seguros		Merger and acquisition	Manufacturing	Financial	Portugal	Europe
2017	Tencent Holdings Ltd.	Snapchat, Inc.	2000.00	Merger and acquisition	Information transmission, computer service and software	Information transmission, computer service and software	USA	North America

(continued)

(continued)

Year	Investor	Counterparty	Transaction amount (million dollars)	Investment method	Industry of investor (first level)	Industry of target	Country/Region of target	Continent
2017	CHN ENERGY Investment Group Co., Ltd.	Copelouzos Group	3520.00	Merger and acquisition	Production and supply of power, gas and water	Production and supply of power, gas and water	Greece	Europe
2017	Suzhou Dongshan Precision Manufacturing Co., Ltd	eASIC Corporation		Merger and acquisition	Manufacturing	Manufacturing	USA	North America
2017	Beijing Bytedance Technology Co., Ltd.	Musical.ly	1000.00	Merger and acquisition	Information transmission, computer service and software	Information transmission, computer service and software	USA	North America
2017	Aa Industrial Belting (Shanghai) Co., Ltd.	Bode Belting GmbH	1.73	Merger and acquisition	Manufacturing	Manufacturing	Germany	Europe
2017	Norinco International Cooperation Ltd.	Energija Projekt d.d.	37.00	Merger and acquisition	Production and supply of power, gas and water	Production and supply of power, gas and water	Croatia	Europe
2017	Guizhou Tyre Co., Ltd.		400.00	Newly-established	Manufacturing	Manufacturing	Vietnam	Asia
2017	Lenovo Group Limited	Fujitsu Global		Merger and acquisition	Manufacturing	Manufacturing	Japan	Asia
2017	China Merchants Group Co., Ltd.		1120.00	Newly-established	Financial	Transportation, storage and post	Sri Lanka	Asia
2017	China Southern Power Grid Company Limited	Brookfield Infrastructure Partners LP	1300.00	Merger and acquisition	Production and supply of power, gas and water	Production and supply of power, gas and water	Chile	South America
2017	Geely Automobile Holdings Ltd.	Volvo Group		Merger and acquisition	Manufacturing	Manufacturing	Sweden	Europe
2017	STATE GRID Corporation of China	CPFL Energia S.A.	6568.58	Merger and acquisition	Production and supply of power, gas and water	Production and supply of power, gas and water	Brazil	South America

(continued)

(continued)

Year	Investor	Counterparty	Transaction amount (million dollars)	Investment method	Industry of investor (first level)	Industry of target	Country/Region of target	Continent
2017	Jiangxi Special Electric Motor Co., Ltd.	Tawana Resources NL	14.79	Merger and acquisition	Manufacturing	Mining	Australia	Oceania
2017	Shanghai Feilo Acoustics Co., Ltd.	Havells Sylvania (Thailand) Limited	1.85	Merger and acquisition	Manufacturing	Manufacturing	Thailand	Asia
2017	Shanghai Feilo Acoustics Co., Ltd.	Feilo Malta Limited	40.00	Merger and acquisition	Manufacturing	Manufacturing	UK	Europe
2017	Zhejiang Dingli Machinery Co., Ltd.	California Manufacturing and Engineering Co., LLC	20.00	Merger and acquisition	manufacturing	Manufacturing	USA	North America
2017	GSR Capital	NEC Corporation	54.00	Merger and acquisition	Financial	Manufacturing	Japan	Asia
2017	C C Land Holdings Limited			Newly-established	Real estate	Real estate	UK	Europe
2017	China Telecom Corporation Limited	OI S.A.		Merger and acquisition	Information transmission, computer service and software	Information transmission, computer service and software	Brazil	South America
2017	China Molybdenum Co., Ltd.	Louis Dreyfus Company Metals B.V.		Merger and acquisition	Mining	Transportation, storage and post		
2017	Suzhou Chunxing Precision Mechanical Co., Ltd.	CALIENT Technologies, Inc.	147.90	Merger and acquisition	Manufacturing	Information transmission, computer service and software	USA	North America
2017	Wolong Electric Group Co., Ltd.	General Electric Company	160.00	Merger and acquisition	Manufacturing	Manufacturing	USA	North America
2017	New Concepts Holdings Limited	Vimab Holding AB	23.55	Merger and acquisition	Construction	Manufacturing	Sweden	Europe
2017	China Resources (Holdings) Co., Ltd.	Dudgeon Offshore Wind Farm	805.00	Merger and acquisition	Comprehensive	Production and supply of power, gas and water	UK	Europe

(continued)

(continued)

Year	Investor	Counterparty	Transaction amount (million dollars)	Investment method	Industry of investor (first level)	Industry of target	Country/Region of target	Continent
2017	Next Capital Ltd.	LithiumX Energy Corp.	206.00	Merger and acquisition	Financial	Production and supply of power, gas and water	Canada	Europe
2017	Nan Fung Group		396.00	Newly-established	Real estate	Real estate	UK	Europe
2017	China Resources (Holdings) Co., Ltd.	NSM Magnettechnik GmbH	4.61	Merger and acquisition	Manufacturing	Manufacturing	Germany	Europe
2017	Shanghai Yunfeng Investment Management Limited	Esaote S.p.A	333.00	Merger and acquisition	Financial	Manufacturing	Italy	Europe
2017	Shenzhen Selen Science & Technology Co., Ltd.	Akron Polymer Systems, Inc.		Merger and acquisition	Manufacturing	Manufacturing	USA	North America
2017	Chen Hsong Holdings Limited			Merger and acquisition	Manufacturing	Real estate	UK	Europe
2017	Golden Meditech Holdings Limited	ASA Global Inc.	7.71	Merger and acquisition	Manufacturing	Real estate	Japan	Asia
2017	Beijing Xiaoju Technology Co., Ltd.	Ride-hailing application 99	100.00	Merger and acquisition	Information transmission, computer service and software	Information transmission, computer service and software	Brazil	South America
2017	Zhejiang Huayou Cobalt Co., Ltd.	Nzuri Copper Limited	7.37	Merger and acquisition	Manufacturing	Mining	Australia	Oceania
2017	Songz Automobile Air Conditioning Co., Ltd.	Bitzer SE	3.80	Merger and acquisition	Manufacturing	Manufacturing	Finland	Europe
2017	Cheung Kei Group	Saïd Holdings	355.70	Merger and acquisition	Real estate	Real estate	UK	Europe
2017	Estun Automation Co., Ltd.	M.A.I GMBH & CO. KG	10.22	Merger and acquisition	Manufacturing	Manufacturing	Germany	Europe

(continued)

(continued)

Year	Investor	Counterparty	Transaction amount (million dollars)	Investment method	Industry of investor (first level)	Industry of target	Country/Region of target	Continent
2017	Tencent Music Entertainment Group	Spotify AB		Merger and acquisition	information transmission, computer service and software	information transmission, computer service and software	Sweden	Europe
2017	Boe Technology Group Co., Ltd.	SES-imagotag	237.00	Merger and acquisition	Manufacturing	Manufacturing	France	Europe
2017	Hefei Metalforming Intelligent Manufacturing Co., Ltd.	Lauffer Pressen GmbH & Co. KG, Maschinenfabrik	27.70	Merger and acquisition	Manufacturing	Manufacturing	Germany	Europe
2017	Geely Automobile Holdings Ltd.	AB Volvo		Merger and acquisition	Manufacturing	Manufacturing	Sweden	Europe
2017	Tempus Investment Holding Co., Ltd.	Trans Maldivian Airways Private Limited	100.00	Merger and acquisition	Comprehensive	Culture, sport and entertainment	Malaysia	Asia
2017	黑龙江飞鹤乳业有限公司	Vitamin World Inc.	28.00	Merger and acquisition	Agriculture, forestry, animal husbandry and fishing	Agriculture, forestry, animal husbandry and fishing	USA	North America
2017	Huaxin Cement Co., Ltd.		140.00	Newly-established	Manufacturing	Construction	Nepal	Asia
2017	Hengli Investments Holding (Group) Limited	25 Gresham Street	210.80	Merger and acquisition	Real estate	Real estate	UK	Europe
2017	King Stone Energy Group Limited	Kuni Umi Energy Co., Ltd.	8.66	Merger and acquisition	Manufacturing	Manufacturing	Japan	Asia
2017	Beijing New Building Materials Public Limited Company	Sunshine Group Ltd.		Newly-established	Manufacturing	Manufacturing	Tanzania	Africa

(continued)

(continued)

Year	Investor	Counterparty	Transaction amount (million dollars)	Investment method	Industry of investor (first level)	Industry of target	Country/Region of target	Continent
2017	Renren Media Holding Ltd.	Trucker Path		Merger and acquisition	Information transmission, computer service and software	Information transmission, computer service and software	USA	North America
2017	Boai Nky Medical Holdings Ltd.	BioVision, Inc.	288.00	Merger and acquisition	Manufacturing	Manufacturing	USA	North America

The manufacturer's authorised representative in the EU is Springer Nature Customer Service Centre GmbH, Europaplatz 3, 69115 Heidelberg, Germany. If you have any concerns regarding our products, please contact ProductSafety@springernature.com

Printed and bound by CPI Group (UK) Ltd, Croydon, CR0 4YY
30/09/2026
02225513-0009